THE AUSTRALIAN GAMBLER'S GUIDE

THE AUSTRALIAN GAMBLER'S GUIDE

Matcham Caine

First published 1991 by
Reed Books Pty Ltd
3/470 Sydney Road
Balgowlah NSW 2093

© 1991 The Watermark Press

All rights reserved. No part of this publication may be reproduced, stored in a retrieval system, or transmitted in any form or by any means, electronic, mechanical, photocopying, recording or otherwise without the prior permission of the publishers.

National Library of Australia
Cataloguing-in-Publication Data

Caine, Matcham
The Australian Gambler's Guide

1. Gambling - Australia. I. Title.

795.0994

Produced in Australia for the Publisher by
The Watermark Press, Sydney

Printed in Singapore by Kyodo Printing

Acknowledgements

Special thanks to Neville Penton, who wrote the section on horse racing and contributed to the section on cheating.

Thanks also to James McCulloch, Danny Gladstone from International Gaming Technology, Telford Conlon and Alan Highfield.

Lastly, we would like to acknowledge the assistance of the various casinos, TABs and state lottery commissions for providing much of the material required to write this book.

CONTENTS

Introduction — 7

Casino Games — 9
- Roulette — 11
  - French Roulette — 20
- Baccarat — 21
- Blackjack — 29
  - Pontoon — 39
- Craps — 41
- Simple Dice Games — 52
- Two-Up — 55

Machine Games — 59
- Poker Machines — 61
- Keno — 69

Racing — 75
- Betting with the Bookies — 77
- Placing a Bet with the TAB — 86
- Other Races — 91
- An A-Z Guide for the Punter — 96

Lotteries — 99

Poker — 109

Backgammon — 129

Cheating — 143

Glossary — 151

Bibliography — 159

INTRODUCTION

There can be little doubt that gambling is one of Australia's favourite pastimes. It seems that no sooner had our ancestors stepped ashore than they were tossing coins in the air or shuffling a pack of cards. Early records of Australian life abound with accounts and descriptions of gambling, whether on the streets, in rusty tin enclosures, on the track, in opium dens or even in Officers' and Gentlemen's clubs. Regardless of race, creed or class, gambling soon became a way, or at least an aspect, of life for many Australians.

Nevertheless, Australia has had a chequered history with gambling, perhaps typified by Two-Up which, despite its resounding popularity, has been played illegally for most of its life. In contrast, we are now experiencing the greatest changes in Australian gambling laws. All states are expected to have legal casinos soon (only NSW and Victoria are still to pass legislation in their favour), and the current trend towards the deregulation of slot machines is expected to continue. It is with this in mind that THE AUSTRALIAN GAMBLER'S GUIDE was published.

Basically there are two types of gambling: those of pure chance and those that require knowledge or skill. Examples of the former include Lotto, Poker machines, Keno and, generally speaking, the casino games. Of the other you would include Poker, Backgammon and horse racing. Punters and bookies especially, spend much time studying the form.

For games of pure chance the main topic of discussion as far as returns are concerned, is the house 'take'. Put in a nutshell, the house take, which applies to ALL games of chance run by a house, is the degree or margin to which that house is guaranteeing its own profit - from your money! Let us take Roulette as an example. With this game there are many bets available but one of them is for either red or black numbers on each spin of the wheel. Even money is offered for these bets which, if there were ONLY red and black numbers, would amount to even returns. But there is also a 0, which is neither a red nor a black number because casinos have to make a profit. Effectively this 0 is the house take.

House margins vary from game to game and even among different bets in the same game: a bet for a single number in Roulette, for example, will return slightly different odds than the example above. The important thing to know here is that if you play long enough you are sure to lose money, that at least is how the statistics work, so when playing casino games select those which give you the best chances. This is largely the aim of the book.

As far as knowledge and skill are concerned they really speak for themselves. Nevertheless the point must be emphasised that against a player (or bookie) with greater knowledge or skill you really do not have a hope of winning, especially if you keep on pitting your inexperience against them. With horses this is obvious but even with Poker many overestimate the role chance plays in winning. Certainly the cards are dealt at random but winning depends more on bluffing and the other techniques. Never forget this.

Other games such as Blackjack may involve some skill despite being primarily games of chance. Card counting, if practicable, may tip the odds slightly in your favour with Blackjack but casinos deter this as much as possible.

Gambling, by definition, is any game where the odds are against you; if the odds were in your favour what you would be doing is investing. So why gamble? Well, as the old adage goes, you have to be in it to win it. Good luck!

CASINO GAMES

ROULETTE

Considered by many to be the definitive casino game, Roulette was invented around the end of the 18th century in France. It soon became established at Monte Carlo and thence spread throughout the world.

'Roulette' itself means 'little wheel' in French — in fact French is the universal language of Roulette although other versions have since been developed which are conducted in English.

The first alternative was invented in America and differs from the French in that instead of only one zero being on the wheel there are two. Because the zeros on the wheels effectively amount to the house edge the American Roulette system consequently takes more from the players. The house edge on the American system works out to just over 5% while on the European it is around half this at 2.7%, and around half this again for even money bets. The advantages of the American system though are that it is faster, and for those who don't speak French much easier.

Australian casinos have adopted their version of the game from the British, itself a combination of the American and French games. Thus the Australian game is fast (though nothing like as frenetic as Craps) and spoken in English while taking from the European version the idea (and fairer odds) of the single zero. But on the subject of odds note that the Australian game doesn't offer a 'prison' (or insurance) for even money bets on zero as the European version does. (See notes on French Roulette on page 20.)

Alongside other casino games such as Blackjack and Craps, Roulette rates a fair to middling on the house edge scale. That is, for an equal stake played over a considerable period of time you are destined, statistically, to lose more money on Roulette than on the other two games. On the other hand, with a bit of luck on your side there is still the possibility of having a windfall at Roulette, by backing the wheel for higher odds. Unlike certain other games in this book, including Craps and Blackjack, the various bets available in Roulette all return nearly the same margins to the punter so that you are not disadvantaged by making the longer bets because the house is offering odds much higher than the probability of getting them. If this is unclear see the section on Craps and in particular the parts explaining the longer odds bets such as Big 6 and Big 8.

Another feature of Roulette is that it lends itself well to systems playing, adding another dimension to the game. Some of these systems have become well known and we'll be discussing those later. But for now let us just look at how the game is played. It is more simple than it looks.

Rules of Roulette

Firstly the colour-coding of the chips used in Roulette is different to other tables: instead of the colours representing values, they represent players. One player may be using red, for instance, another blue and so on. The players select their colour before sitting down, nominating as they do what the chips are worth, according to how much money they hand over. This makes it easy for both the dealer and the players to locate bets.

From here on playing Roulette is simply a matter of placing your chips in one of the areas on the table before the wheel is spun, or even after, if you can get in before the croupier calls 'no more bets'. On page 15 is a sample layout of a table and with it a key to some of the easier and most-used bets. It is simple enough not to need a detailed explanation. Just take particular care when placing the chips on the table to indicate which bet you are making. If you can't reach the appropriate areas you may indicate your preference(s) to the croupier who will place your chips for you. The most efficient way of letting the croupier know what you want is to call out the first and last numbers. For example 'one to four' or 'first four' could only indicate the first corner; 'sixteen to eighteen' the sixth street, and so on.

Additional Bets

Having learnt the series of bets shown in the diagram over the page you may wish to move on to others: there is nothing to prevent you selecting whichever numbers you prefer. There are, however, some additional 'special' bets. The first of these is called a 'final' (or often 'finale') and is a bet on all numbers with the same last digit. Thus 2, 12, 22, 32 etc. In this case 'final two' will be called out to the croupier who will place a chip or chips on each of the relevant numbers. You will notice that finals on 7, 8 and 9 require a minimum of only three chips.

The second set of special bets are known as 'neighbour' bets and are usually favoured by those who believe there may be a mechanical or other bias in the wheel causing the ball to land in a certain section. In fact there is always a bias in a wheel — it is too much to expect them to be perfect — yet despite being infinitesimally small it is enough for some punters to think they can pick it. The most basic form of neighbours betting is to nominate a number to the croupier and at the same time hand over enough chips to cover as many of its neighbours as you wish. Thus if you nominate 'neighbours on 12' and hand the croupier seven chips (or seven units of chips) you will be betting on 12 with 29, 7 and 28 on one side and 35, 3 and 26 on the other. Other bets include neighbours of 0, a third of the wheel (twelve numbers)

BETS AND ODDS

A - 'straight up' on any single number, including 0. Pays 35/1.

B - 'split' covers any one of two numbers. Pays 17/1.

C - 'street' covers any one of three numbers. Pays 11/1.

D - 'corner' covers any one of four numbers. Pays 8/1.

E - 'six line' covers any one of six numbers. Pays 5/1.

F - 'column' covers any one of the three vertical columns. Pays 2/1.

G - 'dozen' covers any of the series of twelve. Pays 2/1.

H - 'even chances'. These pay even money.

I - cover 0, 1, 2 and 3. Pays 8/1

and half the wheel (seventeen numbers).

Lastly there is 'completing a number' which means selecting a number and all the numbers immediately surrounding it on the table layout. Therefore either four, six or nine units are required. The payout from this bet depends on whether the number you have chosen lies in the middle of the table or at the side. See diagram on page 16. If your chip is on a middle number you will receive a payout of 15/1; if a side number (but not one in a far corner) about 14/1. Note that if it is one of the 'off' numbers that comes up you are guaranteed to either break even or make a small profit.

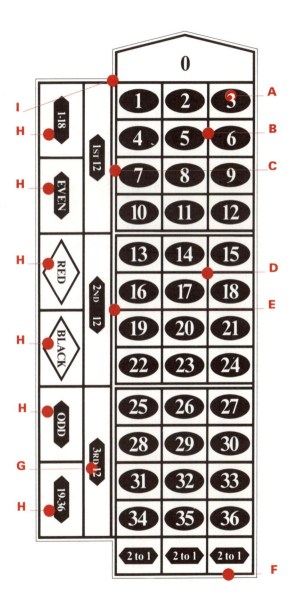

The roulette table

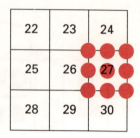

Systems and Strategy

As mentioned earlier a feature of Roulette is that it lends itself well to systems playing. Do not make the mistake of thinking that systems have any bearing on predicting the spin of the wheel. However given some luck in selecting numbers, a system may ensure that your losses are kept to a minimum while taking advantage of your gains. This is really the point of systems. All the systems explained work on the principle of staking on any of the even money bets on the table. That is, for either red or black, odds or evens, 1-18 or 19-36.

You may, incidentally, prefer a more personal way of playing than those given here, such as your children's birthdays or telephone numbers or numerology or whatever, and there is no reason why not: these are all just as logical and can be converted to systems with a little thought.

One other point worth mentioning at this stage concerns the common belief that when, for instance, a sequence of spins turns up a succession of red numbers, then the chances of the next spin turning up a black are greater. The 'law of averages' is often quoted. This is quite correct over a considerable period of time but in the short-term — when the wheel is about to spin — you cannot assume anything. That is, the possibility of black turning up after a sequence of three reds, or three blacks for that matter, or whatever, is the same as on the last throw or any other throw. In mathematical terms each throw is mutually exclusive. This confusion often occurs when the pundit is calculating instead the probability of black turning up after a succession of reds BEFORE any throws have been made. The probability of three reds appearing and then a black is indeed minimal but not relevant here.

The Martingale and Anti-Martingale Systems

These are probably the easiest systems to play and therefore the best for the newcomer. The Martingale consists simply of doubling your stakes when you lose a coup to hopefully retrieve your money the next time around. For example you have two chips placed on the table hoping for red to appear. You lose so now you put down four chips. This time, assuming you win, you have your original two chips back plus another two. You now start at two chips again, and so on. The disadvantage with this system is that with a sequence of losing throws you can quickly start betting excessive amounts of money. Generally it is best to avoid systems or any other staking plans which don't have a cut-out point.

The Anti-Martingale is the reverse of this; you double your stakes after a win. If you lose you drop back to the stake put up before the losing one. The problem here is that the probability of winning enough coups in a row to have enough to cover losing spins is against you. Because of this, the system isn't really practical; to be attempted only when you are feeling lucky.

The Labouchere

This is an interesting system which involves a series of numbers. These, at the same time, determine the number betted on and the stakes put up for it. It is virtually a game within itself: you have lost when you have no more numbers to play (which also controls your losses) and you have won when you can afford to take the day off work! Say you have six numbers, for simplicity's sake; 1, 2, 3, 4, 5, 6. You may have more, or less, it's up to you. The idea is to add the first and last numbers in the sequence and place your chips accordingly, in either the odds or evens areas of the table. The amount you bet is also determined by these numbers. In this example you add 1 and 6 to get 7, an odd number, and you place seven chips (or units) on the odds section of the table. If you win you add the number to your sequence (making it 1, 2, 3, 4, 5, 6, 7) and again bet with the first and last numbers. If you lose you cross 1 and 6 off the list and bet with the next two end numbers: 2 and 5.

The advantage here is that you know in advance how much you will lose if the play goes against you (21 for this sequence). On the other hand I suggest that you draw a cut-out point for your winnings. Four wins straight away, with the six numbers given, will return a windfall of 34 units (7 + 8 + 9 + 10).

Labouchere can also be played in reverse, that is, instead of crossing out numbers when you lose you cross them out when you win. Although less optimistic it is quite playable — just watch that your losses, should you have a run of bad luck, don't go through the roof.

The d'Alembert

This system is best explained by example but the idea is to add a unit to your stakes every time you lose a coup and to subtract one every time you win. Let us take as our example the following series of wins and losses: L W W. Refer to the table over the page.

Here you can see the first spin was lost, so 1 was added

Spin	Stake	Result	Win/Loss
First	1	L	-1
Second	2	W	+1
Third	1	W	+2
Fourth	0	-	-

to the original stake of 1 to provide a stake of 2 for the next spin. This was won so 1 was subtracted from the stake of 2 for the next spin to give 1, and so on. The Win/Loss column shows you how you are progressing with the units used. Two things to note with this method is that every time the stakes go back to 0 you are up in the Win/Loss column (by the amount of the last stake bet) and again if you have a series of losses you can quickly find yourself running out of chips.

With all these systems, and especially with this one, it is a good idea to practice them first at home in order to keep the bets going consistently and smoothly once out in the real thing. Also remember to set cut-out points, both up and down, where required.

Single Numbers

There is of course no reason why any number will appear with more or less frequency in Roulette than any other number, all things being equal (which you can assume they are), so there is no advantage in choosing a 'sleeper' or instead a number very common. People will tend to do so all the same, of course, and if they are winning as a result of it, what can you say? The element of luck, perhaps divine intervention, is one of the mysteries of gambling that keeps people fascinated, or hopeful, or broke. In other words if you believe you are about to hit a lucky streak don't let mere logic stop you. Logic can only do so much.

What I really wanted to say about single numbers though is that there is a belief, apparently supported by research, that single numbers are the best bets for Roulette. Given that the house edge for all bets on the wheel is the same, you can see that with the single numbers there is a 35/1 return on your money. The theory goes that one or two wins with this bet may see you well out in front. On the other hand lots of bets for even money may find you losing less in the short-term but less likely to make a substantial gain.

French Roulette

As I mentioned at the beginning of this section, the Australian table is an indirect hybrid of the French (or European) and American tables. However, in at least one Australian casino there is the option of playing the French version, generally considered the most aristocratic of Roulette games. Here all calls are made in French, the table signs are written in French and croupiers use rakes to move the chips. The game is played with some pomp and ceremony with players seated on both sides of the table. It is much slower than the standard game of Roulette played in Australia and probably averages only half as many turns of the wheel in an hour. Otherwise it is very similar.

The principal difference between them is that when zero comes up in the French version all stakes in the even money areas may be placed 'en prison' (in prison). Then the wheel is spun again to determine their fate. If the wheel falls in your favour this time you keep your chips; if not you lose them.

BACCARAT

Baccarat, first played in Europe over five hundred years ago, is one of the classic casino games played in various forms in casinos around the world. All these forms are basically very similar; the cards are played in a similar fashion, but the way the bank is handled varies markedly. For example in the version called Chemin de Fer the banker sets the wager for the hand (or 'coup') and a volunteer from amongst the other players is called upon to play against the banker. Thus the game is primarily on a one-to-one basis. With Baccarat Banque the bank is held by the venue and the coup is made with players on two tables betting against it. There is also another version known as Mini-Baccarat which looks a little like Blackjack and is played in several casinos in Australia. Otherwise the version we play here is based on the game of Punto Banco, where the bank is passed around the table to each player in turn (the banker being the person holding the shoe) while the players bet against the fall of the cards only.

Whatever the case, Baccarat is a game of glamour and high stakes. For one thing it affords those with the desire to be in the spotlight their chance to do so, however discreet the actual lighting may be. Another aspect of Baccarat is that the game has a ritualistic quality about it, moving slowly and deliberately through the coups. It has the distinction of being a class act.

Although the stakes often go quite high in Baccarat it is worth noting that, like Blackjack, it is considered to be a very fair game in that the house edge is low. Also, because there are basically only two ways you can bet, both with very equal chances of winning and both for even money, the opportunity to be 'taken for a ride' is virtually eliminated (but see later). One can therefore be assured that unless an incredible amount of ill-luck falls your way, or you bet in greater amounts than you can afford, then you are not likely to be excessively down at the end of the day. For beginners this is perhaps even more the case with Baccarat than with Blackjack, because here skill is not really an element of the game.

How to Play

Once the cards have been shuffled by the croupier and cut they are passed to the banker who, at the beginning of the day's play would be the first person on the right of the croupier. The cards are contained within a shoe. The banker then deals two cards, alternately, to 'Players' and 'Bank' which in this sense doesn't refer to anyone sitting around the table but to areas set aside for the deal. The croupier then calls the total of the two cards and directs the banker to draw another card or not for each of the two hands according to the set rules of the game. Only one extra card, if any, is drawn for each hand.

In the meantime the players and the banker have placed their bets in the areas provided, either for Bank or Players, to win the coup. Note that bets may be made regardless of the punter's current status (thus the banker can bet on Players and vice versa). What they are hoping for is that the total of their chosen hand is closer to 9 than the other. If so they of course win. The totals are calculated as follows:

All cards are valued according to their numerical value, so that a 2 is worth 2 and so on. Face cards (K, Q, J, A) and 10s are worth 0. Any combination of cards equalling 10 also counts as 0. You have then, for example, 6 + 4 = 0 but 6 + 4 + 4 = 4 and 7 + 2 = 9 but 7 + 5 + 3 = 5 and K + 6 = 6. Under this system it is not possible for a hand to go bust.

Let us now play an imaginary game. The first two cards have been dealt and you are wondering whether a third card is following for each hand. The tables given below show clearly and finally if it will or won't be. After the totals are added and a winning hand declared the croupier makes the appropriate payouts.

Player	
With a total of	
1,2,3,4,5,6,10	Draws a card
6,7	Stands
8,9	Natural

Banker		
With a total of	*Draws when giving*	*Does not draw when giving*
3	1,2,3,4,5,6,7,9,10	8
4	2,3,4,5,6,7	1,8,9,10
5	4,5,6,7	1,2,3,8,9,10
6	6,7	1,2,3,4,5,8,9,10
7	Stands	
8,9	Natural	

Here the croupier, representing the Player's hand draws a third card when scoring a total on the first two cards of 1,2,3,4,5 or 10, stands when those cards equal 6 or 7, and wins outright (unless stand-off, see text) on 8 or 9. The Banker draws a third card depending on the third card given to Players. Thus with a total of a 6 or 7 the Banker will only draw a card if the Player's third card is a 6 or 7, and so on.

In counting the values of the cards a score of 8 or 9 on the first two cards is called a 'natural' and wins outright unless the other hand also has a natural in which case a stand-off is called and the banker is asked to deal again. However a natural of 9 beats a natural of 8. Equal scores also comprise a stand-off and the same conditions apply. Remember that the croupier calls all actions in the game so it is not necessary to memorise the table or rules.

Lastly, you will see on the layout of the table a section marked 'Tie'. This gives you the option of betting on a stand-off, at 8/1 as also marked on the table. It is not recommended though because at these odds the house is sitting on a healthy edge of around 14%. Since the normal house edge is around 1%, why take the risk?

The Banker

As I mentioned earlier the bank is passed anti-clockwise around the table. All seated players have the right to become the banker when it is their turn but doing so is optional. Also, the banker can forfeit his or her turn at will. That is, you don't have to wait until you lose to resign as banker. Otherwise you lose the bank when the Players hand wins that round. A marked card indicates that the pack is almost through and it is then shuffled before being handed back to the bank. There are usually six packs of cards in a shoe.

It should be noted that the game of Baccarat is only played when a sufficient number of people express an interest. The casino will decide whether it is worthwhile setting up a table.

The Layout of the Table

Looking at the illustration over the page you will notice that there are numbered positions which correspond to the seated players. Between them on one side sits the croupier and on the other side two dealers who handle the bets. Chips are placed in the areas marked 'Players' or 'Bank'. Additionally you may place your bet in the 'Tie' area at the top. And that is really all there is to know about the table except that the additional boxes in the centre marked 1, 2, 3 etc. are for the dealers to work out how much each player owes the house in commission. We'll discuss this aspect in the next section on payouts.

One other thing to add at this stage though is that you don't have to be seated to bet. If you are standing and the seated player in front of you is not making a bet for that round you are entitled to use his or her space. You are not however entitled to the bank.

Payouts

As mentioned earlier winning bets are paid even money. There is a qualification to this however; winning Bank

---

MINI BACCARAT

This is played according to the same rules as Baccarat, the differences being that a smaller table, like a Blackjack table, is used and only the croupier handles the cards. There are seven seats and the table is marked with a spot each for Bankers and Players. There are also boxes for the commission (a 5% commission applies here as well as for the larger Baccarat) and an additional tie bet at odds of 8/1. Like Baccarat, this tie bet gives the house an edge of 14% so it is not advised.

The appeal of Mini-Baccarat, especially for the newcomer to the game, is that it is easier than its big brother. It is also faster.

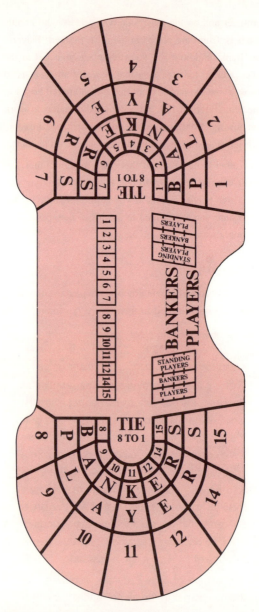

The layout of the Baccarat table

bets are subject to a commission of 5% to the bank. This is not paid immediately after each coup but either at the end of the shoe, when the cards are being reshuffled, or when the player leaves the game. In the meantime the dealers are placing tokens in the numbered squares provided on the table to keep count. I suggest you keep an eye on them so you are not caught short at the end.

At this point, having noted that both hands pay out even money, you may be building a case towards betting in favour of either the Bank or Players, having also noted that both hands are playing under slightly different handicaps: the 5% commission in the case of the Bank and the shortened draw in the case of Players (see page 26). Surely the net sum of these handicaps is an advantage to one of the hands? This is in fact the case, but the difference, in favour of the Bank, only amounts to around 0.2% which is hardly worth taking into consideration.

In conclusion it should be noted that the 5% levy to the house is not the same thing as the house edge. To calculate the edge you have to estimate what hands the players are losing to the house over a period of time, then take into account the levy. Because both hands are very equally matched and the payout for both is even money (or very near) the actual house edge, which is only around 1%, is by casino standards very low indeed making Baccarat one of the best games available.

How to Win

There is little you can do to improve your chances at Baccarat (except by betting in favour of the Bank for the slightly higher edge) as the game is entirely one of chance. Superstition and/or luck may play their parts (why is it that one banker always draws winning Player's hands while another always loses them?) but otherwise there is only card counting left as a method and this isn't practical. More to the point the way the cards fall early in the game makes no difference to the comparative advantage of each hand. There is a belief however that if plenty of 5s appear early it is to the Bank's advantage, and the reverse works for the Players. Since calculations have proven this to be true it could be worth watching for runs of this number.

BLACKJACK

The distinct advantage Blackjack has over other forms of casino gambling is that it is the one most likely to be familiar to the newcomer. Even if it is only Pontoon they have played (to distinguish it here from Blackjack) the rules are sufficiently similar to enable them to walk straight up to a table and begin playing. This in part accounts for Blackjack being the most popular casino game, although other factors, such as the control the players have over their own hands and the slower pace of the game, which allows some conversation between plays, also contribute.

Another major source of its popularity is that it is the game which returns the best odds to the punter, assuming some skill is employed in playing the hands — a fact which has not gone unnoticed amongst serious players. These skills involve knowing, or at least 'guesstimating' when to draw and when not to as well as when to 'split' and when not to, and so on. Skills may also be employed in counting cards, a controversial point discussed later. Even with only a little skill however one is fairly safe, as the rules of Blackjack do to a certain extent protect the player from making decisions they may later regret.

There are two basic versions of Blackjack played in casinos worldwide, with some variations. They are known as the 'London deal' and the 'Nevada deal' and in Australia we play the former. The difference between the two games is that in the London deal the cards are dealt face up whereas it is the reverse in the Nevada version. Another difference is that with the London deal the dealer takes his or her second card only after all the players have finished playing their hands. In the Nevada deal both cards are dealt initially. These differences call for slightly varying strategies although in all other ways the games are identical.

We will be looking only at the London deal in this book.

How to Play

The object of Blackjack is to score a hand as close as possible to 21 without going over it. This is done by drawing cards from the dealer, as many as you have the nerve for. If you go over (exceed 21) you 'bust', meaning you have automatically lost the hand.

Against this the dealer is also trying to score a hand as close as possible to 21 without going over. Whoever has the highest hand wins. If you are both sitting on equal scores at the end a 'stand-off' is called and all bets are carried on to the next hand. Thus any one player is competing directly and only against the dealer even though there may be other players at the table. The basic play is at even money.

Each card then (standard packs of playing cards are used) is assigned a certain value. Aces are worth 1 or 11 depending on how you wish to use them, face cards (K, Q, J) are worth 10 and all other cards are worth whatever their numerical value.

Each player is first dealt two cards, face up, and the dealer one. Starting from the left of the table the players in turn either 'stand' or 'draw' depending on their hands and their confidence. Each player can draw as many cards as they wish until they 'bust'. When all players have finished playing the hands the dealer draws and the game is decided.

This is the basic game and really there isn't much more to it than that, except the strategy required to win. But note the additional plays described later.

Blackjack

A Blackjack is any hand of two cards which contains an Ace and a face card or 10. It automatically wins the hand for the player or dealer concerned, unless both player (or players) and dealer have Blackjacks in which case a stand-off is called. In a stand-off all money is left on the table until the next play, except for the money of those players without Blackjack, who all lose. A winning Blackjack wins a payout of 3/2 for a winning player or whatever money is on the table for the house. A Blackjack is also known as a 'natural'.

An example of a Blackjack.

Insurance

When the dealer's first hand is an Ace the players can insure against him or her having a Blackjack by placing up to half their current stakes in the insurance area provided. This is in effect an additional bet and covers the player against their own hand losing. Thus if the dealer does draw a Blackjack the player will win on the dealer's hand while losing on their own. The exception to this is if the player also draws a Blackjack in which case a stand-off is called. Here you will keep your initial bet while still winning insurance money. Insurance is paid at 2/1. If the dealer doesn't draw a Blackjack all money placed in insurance is taken by the bank. The down-side of this arrangement is that the odds are well and truly in favour of the house. Consequently, the best advice to give here is to avoid Insurance unless you are sure that there is a very good chance that the dealer will pick up a face card on the next draw, that is, if you have reason to believe there are plenty of these cards left in the pack.

Hard and Soft Hands

A 'hard' hand is one in which there are either no Aces or where the ace counts as a 1 only. If it were to be counted as 11 the hand would be bust. A 'soft' hand is one in which the Ace can be counted as either 1 or 11 depending on your need. For example if you are dealt a 4 and an Ace your hand would be worth 5 or 15. You may decide to draw again. Assuming you draw a 6 your hand would now be worth either 11 or 21 in which case you would nominate the Ace as 11 and 'stand': 21 is the best you can do. If you have two Aces in your hand each can be counted as different values. If your first two cards are an ace and a 10 (or facecard) the Ace is automatically counted as 11 to make the Blackjack.

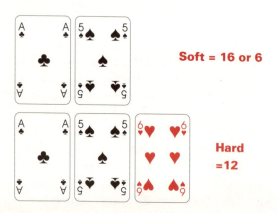

Examples of a soft and hard hand.

A Blackjack table.

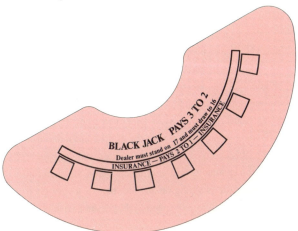

Splitting

The option to split is available to the player when the first two cards make a pair. If taken the player then has two hands to play with, the stake on the second hand made up to match that on the first. The dealer will then place a second card on the first hand to complete the play on that hand before moving on to the next. If they are Aces you are splitting you may draw only one more card for each. Also, if you draw a 10 or face card for either of these Aces then that hand counts as 21 only, not Blackjack. Consequently even money is paid out if you win the hand, not 3/2. In the London deal proper, splitting is not allowed on 4s, 5s and 10s, the reason being to prevent the unknowing punter from making a decision they will live to regret. In other words, splits on these numbers are unlikely to win. This rule is not in place in Australia so take the hint. For an explanation as to why certain numbers are better bets than others refer to the section Playing to Win.

Doubling

Here the Australian system is more like the traditional London deal in that doubling is only allowed on 9s, 10s and 11s. Again, this is for the player's protection. When your first two cards total one of the numbers above doubling allows you to increase your stakes by the same amount again. If you feel there is a good chance of a 10 or facecard appearing with your next draw then it is perhaps a sound idea to take the option, but remember that in this case you are allowed to draw only one more card. Basic strategy will also dictate that if the dealer in the meantime is sitting on an Ace there is a very good chance you will lose the hand, so better not to risk it.

The Deal

The typical Blackjack table consists of seven squares (or 'boxes') for betting, an Insurance area, a 'shoe' (which contains the cards —anywhere from five to eight packs), chips (bought from the dealer prior to the commencement of the game) and the card playing area. There are also seven seats for the players. For each square three bets are allowed so that as well as the seated player two others, standing behind, can play. These people are not dealt cards but bet on the hands of the player seated in front of them. They of course are at the mercy of the way that person plays.

The first thing to check when approaching a table is the minimum and maximum bets permissible: anywhere from $2 upwards usually. Then its a matter of selecting a seat, assuming there are choices available. For a few people seating is very important, perhaps because they feel luckier in some positions, or perhaps because they feel those in the end seats have more time to make up their minds, particularly if they are card counters. This last point may or may not be the case since most experienced players can look at the cards and make their decisions immediately, based on what 'formula' they think will work best for them.

The next stage is to convert whatever money you are willing to bet into chips. Money is simply handed over the table and the appropriate number of chips returned. If it is a new game at that table or you happen to come in when the cards are being shuffled you may be asked to cut the pack.

The cards are then dealt and finally the completed hands are laid out on the table. What is the dealer going to do? Although playing the same game as you the dealer has no choice but to stand or draw according to house rules. That is, on any total of 17 or above the dealer has to stand; on any total less than this the dealer has to draw. It is against this knowledge that serious gamblers are making a plan of attack, balancing the total of their cards against the likely outcome of the dealer's given, remember, that they are looking at the dealer's first card from the time of the initial deal. We will be touching on this point again later in respect to strategy.

Signals

Part of the beauty of Blackjack is that it can be played in almost total silence, with a suitable air of ceremony or ritual, if you are exhausted by conversation. Various universal signals facilitate this. It must be stressed though that their use is not essential — if you are unfamiliar with them or prefer to voice your wishes instead, do so.

'Stand' is indicated by moving your hand sideways over the cards with your fingers stretched out towards the dealer. 'Draw' is indicated by pulling your hand towards you over the cards. If you were voicing your intentions you would just say 'stand' or 'draw' or anything which is otherwise clear to the dealer. For splitting and doubling you have to voice your intentions in Australian casinos because you are not permitted to touch your cards. You then separate your chips and add your extra bets accordingly. Incidentally, the dealer will often ask you if you wish to split or double as the options arise, or if you are new to the game. Any signals misinterpreted by the dealer and acted upon will be referred to an adjudicator should there be any dispute.

Playing to Win

The basic strategy for winning a Blackjack hand, or indeed to winning overall, is to play the optimum hand against the dealer's first card. This involves comparing the value of your own cards with the possibility of what the dealer will score given their first card. For example if your cards total 16 and the dealer's first card is a 10 you may decide to draw again simply because with this as a first card the dealer has a good chance of drawing a number greater than six with no chance of busting. On the other hand if the dealer drew a 4 on the first card you may decide not to draw again because of the possibility of busting against the odds of them either busting or scoring less than 16. Remember that the dealer is

---

BLACKJACK - VIDEO STYLE

Most casinos now also have Blackjack available as a slot game, the rules are similar to the real game of Blackjack except that the stakes are set lower and, in most cases, the house take is higher (around 10%). The exception to this rule is Tasmania where a modified version of the game sees the return to the punter being almost as high as on the real thing , the take is around 2.4%

bound by house rules as to whether they draw or not and this is vital information to the knowing player. For even more information readers should consult Charles Einsteins' HOW TO WIN AT BLACKJACK, a book published in the USA that utilises computerized research findings to determine just what are the optimum hands against the dealer's first card.

The second basic strategy to winning at Blackjack, which was described in the introduction to this chapter as being controversial, is counting cards. There are different ways this can be done (the most complicated of which involves assigning a value to each of the cards, again, see Einstein's book) but there are also many problems with the method and finally they add up to it being unworkable, or nearly so. I mention it because even if you can't apply these principles arithmetically you are still 'counting' in the sense that you have to guess what will come up next. Consequently this information should still prove of use.

The first problem is that while counting cards is not in fact illegal it is certainly frowned upon in casinos and anyone caught doing it may be banned, at worst, or at least subject to some very cold service. Strangely enough this usually seems to work — players, despite themselves, are very susceptible to intimidation by the house and can often be 'psyched' out.

The second problem is that Blackjack in Australia is played with a shoe containing five to eight packs of cards. This is largely to prevent just such an event occurring. In the past, and in some private games, Blackjack has been and still is played with only one pack of cards. A gift! And although with four packs counting is still a proposition, with eight the memory is being stretched to enormous limits.

Counting works on the principle that in a pack of 52

cards roughly half are 'low' cards (2, 3, 4, 5, 6, 7) and roughly half are 'high' (the rest). If you have reason to believe there are more 'high' cards left in the pack then you know you are more likely to get stronger hands. You therefore bet up. You also know that if you get a 'stiff' (cards totalling 12 to 16 where you can go bust on the next draw) it is better probably to stand. This is because the odds are that you will draw a 'low' card. You can then lower your betting accordingly.

The most simple form of counting and the only one we shall discuss here is where you only keep track of the 10s and face cards coming out of the shoe until a pattern establishes itself. This pattern will take a long time to calculate in an eight pack shoe but you count on there being an unbiased pack approximately a third of the time, a 'high' pack a third of the time and a 'low' pack a third of the time. Once you know what you are dealing with, start juggling your chips.

There is an opposing view to this which is that if the cards are going to turn up high for you they are also

HIGH ROLLERS

The competition between casinos is strong, particularly when it comes to the 'high rollers' who travel the world gambling scene as a matter of course and bet in millions. These players earn themselves free air tickets as well as free accommodation. Whether they get a hotel suite and first-class airfare depends on how much money they agree to convert into chips. These 'high rollers' are mostly found through referrals by other players.

likely to turn up high for the dealer. So far so good but the dealer (to make the point yet again) is bound by house rules, that is, to draw on cards less than 16 and stand on cards 17 or greater. Therefore they are not in a position to work the pack.

The key then is to bet according to the run of the game. As a guide, consider doubling your money when the play is in your favour. At all other times hold back your betting to your minimum wager. This is a fairly safe approach, perhaps appropriate to any simple counting technique. If you are more confident as to the make up of the pack you may consider trebling or even quadrupling your basic bet. Good luck!

Pontoon

Although the names 'Pontoon' and 'Blackjack' are in fact interchangeable for most (as is the name '21'), a distinction is made here between the game played in casinos and that played in the home. The rules vary on a few points, mostly to enable the casino to make its profit but otherwise the games are played in much the same way. Here I will be explaining only the differences, so refer to the rules of play given earlier in this chapter if you are starting from scratch.

Unlike casino Blackjack the bank changes hands in Pontoon so that every player has the opportunity to exploit its advantage which is that all winning hands tied with the bank go to the bank. There are various methods used for doing this but the most popular one is to give it to the player scoring a natural (or Pontoon). Other methods include passing it on to the next person around the table after each shuffle and passing it on again after a period of time, ten minutes, say. With the first method if two players score Pontoon the bank will go to the player who was dealt it first. If a player does not want to take the bank they may auction it to the highest bidder.

Usually one card is dealt first and the players' stakes are laid on the table. Then each player in turn is asked whether they want to 'buy' a card, 'twist' a card or 'stand'. Bought cards will cost you anything up to the original stake and are dealt face down; twisted cards cost nothing but are dealt face up for the bank to see. Busted hands should be laid face up on the table to show you are out. Once a player has asked for a twist they can no longer buy cards: they are locked into their current stake. Splits may be allowed depending on what the group decides. Usually a Pontoon won't be allowed on split cards. And finally, the player hitting Pontoon in most games is paid double their stakes unless the bank has a Pontoon too in which case a stand-off is called. Pontoons are turned over straight away.

One variation of Pontoon is the 'five-card trick'. This beats any 21, including the bank's, but not a Pontoon. A five-card trick is when a player scores 21 or less with five cards. That person is paid double. In Pontoon, as with Blackjack, each player is playing directly against the bank. Except for the cases given above, payouts by the bank to the winning players are at even money. The bank keeps all stakes of those players who have either busted or scored less. If the bank busts the bank loses and must pay players with valid hands. Players who have also busted may retain their stakes.

CRAPS

This game involves betting on two regular dice which are bounced against a back wall. It is therefore a game of chance; the only skill lies in calculating the odds either for or against a particular throw taking place and betting accordingly. Perhaps an additional skill lies in not getting so caught up in the game that risks are taken against your better judgment. This is very easy to do as the game is both noisy and exciting.

The origin of the game lies in England with a game called Hazard. This was played with a cup from which the caster threw two dice and then took bets on whether he or she could match the total of those dice with a subsequent throw. The caster lost if in the meantime a 2 or a 3 was thrown. The game, in a slightly different form, then moved to New Orleans in the early 1800s. Later, the idea of a bank was introduced and it is in this final form, or something like it, that the game is played in casinos today. Private Craps (without a bank) is still played in some places, most conspicuously by hustlers on street corners in American cities.

As far as casino games go the odds on Craps are quite good — if you can keep to the safest bets. Otherwise the odds against you can lengthen considerably. And if Craps at first sight appears complicated, be reassured that it isn't — it just looks that way because of the layout of the board. Consequently being familiar with the many different types of bets is the key to the game although in practice you can get away with knowing only one or two of them. (You are probably better off too, but we'll come to that point later.) Normal casino chips are used for betting.

On the subject of boards note that there are basically two versions played in casinos, one British and the other

American. The differences between them are slight but worth taking note of because they amount to substantial changes in the odds. Some of these differences will be covered in detail later, when the different types of bets available are explained. The Australian board is a hybrid of the two, although probably closer to the British version. In general this is a good move by the Australian casino industry, at least for the punters, as the British version returns much better odds than the American which in its extremes can even be misleading as to what you are up against. Those concessions made to the American system are all in the bank's favour!

Getting Started

A Craps game involves a 'crew' (the casino staff operating the game), the players (or punters) and a 'shooter' who is selected from amongst the players to roll the dice. The game begins when the 'stickman' (one of the crew) calls on a shooter to select their pair of dice and make the first throw, known as the Come Out roll. What the shooter is rolling for is a 7 or 11. If they are successful even money is returned for whatever bet is made and they move on to the second throw. But if Craps is thrown instead (a 2, 3 or 12) they lose and stand aside for the next shooter who is ordinarily the next player to the left. A player is not obliged to become the shooter.

Any other number thrown becomes a point which means the shooter is now betting on that number being rolled again before a 7. If it does they will receive even money and be entitled to move on to the other rolls. If not, again the shooter forfeits the right to the dice. Note that when attempting a point the shooter loses on a throw of 7 only, not 11, 2, 3 or 12. The shooter must bet on the Come Out roll, either for Win or Don't Win (sometimes Pass or Don't Pass) — its up to them.

In the meantime the players (standing around the outside of the board) are placing wagers on the Win or Don't Win line for the Come Out roll. The bets are placed in the appropriate areas, clearly marked on the table. Gambling is at even money in both cases. This is the easiest place for newcomers entering the game; but players can join the action at any stage. One thing to remember at this point though is that those players betting on the Don't Win line are entitled to re-claim their stakes after the initial point is made — a practice not allowed for any other bet. This is to be discouraged however as once a point has been established the chances of Don't Win players going on to win are at very good odds. The table on page 45 shows the possible combinations of any one throw and the odds against any one number coming up. Here you can see there are more chances of throwing a 7 than any other number.

POKER DICE

Poker dice is a quick game requiring almost no skill but providing lots of amusement. It is well suited to bars or other places where a few friends gather to chat or kill some time. There are five dice, each marked with an Ace, a King, a Queen, a Jack, a 10 and a 9. Suits don't count; instead you are shooting for five of a kind, fours, full house, straight, threes, two pairs and one pair. The rules are similar to Draw poker: one roll and then another with whatever dice you don't want to keep from the first. Each player usually puts up an equal stake - winner takes all. Sometimes a third roll is allowed, depending on who you are playing with.

Note that if a 2 (or on some boards a 12) appears on the initial throw a stand-off is called for those players on the Don't Win line. This means that while the Win liners have lost their bets, the Don't Win liners haven't won. Hence they win on a 3 or 12 only, assuming the stand-off number is 2. The same applies for Don't Come bets (see this page) when a point is yet to be established.

The Come Out roll is just one of the many throws made in Craps; after it is completed any of the other bets described hereupon can be made at any one time by the players. The shooter continues as before until a 7 is thrown, when they must retire. Note that after the Come Out roll the shooter can only lose a bet when 'crapping out' (2, 3 or 12), not the right to continue as thrower.

Come and Don't Come Bets

This is played the same way as the above Win or Don't Win throw and pays the same odds. Thus, only the terminology differs. But see the section Playing to Win to find out how a series of successive points (known as a 'streak') may be played on these bets.

Hard Ways

Here you are betting that for any given Hard Way number (either 4, 6, 8 or 10) the dice will fall on either a 2-2, 3-3, 4-4 or 5-5 before the total of that given number falls by another combination or a 7 is thrown. For example, if you nominate 8 as your number you want a 4-4 before a 5-3, 6-2, 7-1 or any combination adding up to 7 is thrown. The payout is high, 7/1 for a 4 or 10 and 9/1 for a 6 or 8, but the odds of achieving this are minimal, especially when you take into account that there is only one way of throwing a 4-4 but two ways of throwing a 5-3 (5-3 or 3-5) etc. The house edge averages about 10% for Hard Ways. This is an unnecessarily high risk.

Combinations of two dice		
Total on dice	Number of ways	Odds against
2	1	35/1
3	2	17/1
4	3	11/1
5	4	8/1
6	5	31/5
7	6	5/1
8	5	31/5
9	4	8/1
10	3	11/1
11	2	17/1
12	1	35/1

One Roll Bets

Here the player takes odds on a particular number or numbers appearing on the next throw. See table on page 48 for examples of what are the most common bets.

Field Bets

This is another form of the One-Roll bet. The Field comprises the numbers 2, 3, 4, 9, 10, 11 or 12. Even money is paid out if the dice fall on one of the middle numbers; double if the dice lands on a 2 or a 12. The house take on this is just over 5%.

Horn Bets

Yet another One-Roll bet. Combines Eleven, Craps 2, Craps 3 and Craps 12 bets to pay out 7.5/1 if a 2 or a 12 is thrown or 3.5/1 if a 3 or an 11 is thrown. Any other number thrown: you lose. A variation on this is the Horn

High bet which is divided into five parts: one unit (or chip) on each of three numbers and two units (or chips) on your fourth choice.

Place Bets

A Place bet can be made after a point is established and is done by selecting a number from 4, 5, 6, 8, 9 or 10 in numbered boxes shown on the board. Two options are available: a Right Place bet or a Wrong Place bet. With a Right Place bet you are betting that that number will come up before a 7 is thrown; with a Wrong Place bet you are betting that the 7 will come up before your chosen number. The payout varies depending on which number you have chosen and whether you are placing a Right or Wrong Place Bet. See table below for odds.

Numbers 6 and 8 pay 7/6; numbers 5 and 9 pay 7/5 and numbers 4 and 10 pay 9/5, assuming you are going for

Odds on Place Bets		
Right Place Bets		
Bet	Odds	House Take
6 or 8	7/6	1.5%
5 or 9	7/5	4%
4 or 10	9/5	6.8%
Wrong Place Bets		
Bet	Odds	House Take
6 or 8	4/5	1.8%
5 or 9	5/8	2.5%
4 or 10	5/11	3%

the Right Place bet. For Wrong Place bets the payout is structured differently: 4/5 for a 6 or 8, 5/8 for 5 and 9, and 5/11 for the 4 or 10. Of these the best bet mathematically is the first; a bet on 6 or 8 the Right Way, because the house advantage is only 1.52% compared to 6.67% for example on the Right Way bet for 4 or 10.

In order to make payouts easier to facilitate with Place bets it is best to lay down chips in multiples consistent with the odds paid out. So if you are betting the Right Way on a 6 or 8 bet in multiples of five, for example. A Wrong Way bet on a 5 or 9 will be easiest in multiples of eight. The easiest way to remember this is to bet in multiples of whatever is the last number mentioned in the odds.

Big 6 and Big 8 Bets

This is a bet acquired from the American system which demonstrates the point made earlier that the American version of the game has some dubious aspects. Big 6 and Big 8 are played exactly the same way as Place bets where either a 6 or an 8 is chosen as your number. The difference, and it is the only difference between them, is that in this bet the payout is at even money (the bank's edge is about 9%) whereas with a Place bet on a 6 or 8 the payout is 7-6 (Bank edge is 1.52%). This bet is not allowed in the British version of the game. Take the hint.

The Craps Board

In the illustration on the next page you will see a typical layout of an Australian board. The first thing you will notice is that it is in two halves with an additional box (known as a proposition or 'prop' box) in the middle. Don't be confused by this: the layout is designed to facilitate a number of players betting at the one time.

The different areas of the box correspond to the different bets. If you have been following the description of the game so far you will notice some familiar terms. In fact the board should make sense at this point. All that is required is to place your chips in whatever area corresponds to the type of bet you wish to make. For example if there is a new shooter all bets will be placed on either the Win or Don't Win line. Once this has been established you may choose to place your chips in the Come or Don't Come areas, the Field area, the Big 6 or Big 8, or in one of the areas marked in the proposition box.

The numbers across the left of the illustration (that is, 4, 5, 6, 8, 9 and 10) refer to the point being played, when relevant. A 'buck' is placed on that number by the stickman. Note also that the stickman will move any bets from the Come and Don't Come areas to these boxes after the relevant point has been established. Come bets are moved to the bottom half of the point squares; Don't Come bets to the top. Place bets go here as well; they are placed on the double lines running through the middle of the square. The pairs of dice positioned around the board showing a total of 2 (sometimes 12) indicate where stand-offs occur in the game. See the section 'Getting Started' if you are unsure what a stand-off is.

One Roll Bets		
Bet	*Wins on throw of*	*Pays*
Any Craps	2, 3, or 12	7.5/1
Craps 2	2 only	33/1
Craps 3	3 only	16/1
Craps 12	12 only	33/1
Any 7	7	4/1
Eleven	11 only	16/1

CRAPS

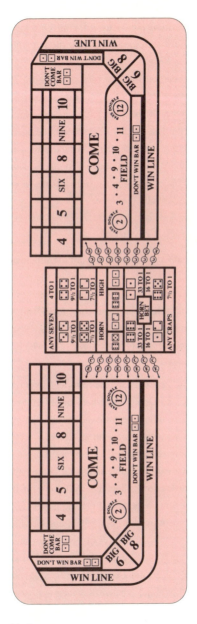

Craps table layout

The proposition box is used for all One-Roll bets including Hard Ways. Starting from the left, chips placed in the 'Any Seven' area receive 4/1 for any 7 thrown, as explained earlier; the next two areas are for Hard Way bets; the next four in a line for Horn High bets; the next four for One-Off bets (including an area for the Horn bet) and the last for any Craps combination. Next to it the (C) circles are additional Any Craps symbols and the (E) circles are additional 11s symbols. The proposition box may vary slightly from casino to casino but remains essentially the same.

Playing To Win

Winning at Craps requires a mixture of luck and care in calculating the odds of the throw of the dice. Luck is always hard to account for — perhaps the best advice is to bet it up when you are feeling lucky and hold back when you know you are losing. As far as calculating the odds are concerned here are some rules which are worth considering.

Firstly, the best bets are the Win and Don't Win bets, the Come and Don't Come bets and Place betting on 6 or 8. This is simply because the house edge over you is less with these bets than with the others — considerably so, the long shots with Craps are well against you, as pointed out earlier. Ignore the fact that the payouts with these bets are low compared with some of the wilder throws — you are better off placing larger stakes on the ones just mentioned, or playing a 'streak' which is running up a long succession of bets when the dice are falling your way. You may be interested to know also that Don't Win and Don't Come bets are marginally (but only marginally) better than their opposites.

A Streak is played by moving from the Come area to as many Point boxes as possible in succession. For example,

FIRST AUSTRALIAN CASINO

The first Australian casino to open was Wrest Point Casino in Hobart in 1973. Thereafter, all Australian casinos have adopted their methods of handling money, instituted to prevent the Mafia-type problems found overseas. This means that every day in every casino all money - cash money - is counted and micro-filmed in the presence of government officials in special rooms. In particular this prevents 'skimming', the practice of raking off money from the top before it has been entered into the ledgers. It is archaic (not to mention time-consuming) perhaps to count every single coin the casino has made at the end of the day, but in that it has helped keep the industry clean and critics quiet it is undoubtedly of some worth.

you are in the Come area when a point of 8 comes up — your chips are moved to the 8 point box. Now you place another bet in the Come area. The shooter throws a 6 and your chips are moved to the 6 Point box. This goes on until hopefully all the points are covered before a 7 is thrown. If so you win with any 'long hand' thrown. However if not the entire series is lost, except for what might be in the Come box. The reverse can also be played, that is, Don't Come bets are made so that every time a 7 is thrown you win.

SIMPLE DICE GAMES

Simply referred to as 'sucker' dice by American gamblers because they require no skill and generally offer relatively poor chances of winning, these games, including Mini-Dice, Sic-Bo, Tai-Sai and Big and Small, are played in all casinos in Australia. However Sic-Bo, Tai-Sai and Big and Small are the same game under different titles so that there are, in practice, only two forms of the game with most casinos offering one or the other.

Whichever form is offered though and despite the high house takes in both, the lure is that it is possible to win odds of up to 190/1, resulting in a large payout for a very small sum of money.

Both games involve drawing three dice from either a spinning cage known as a 'chuck' cage or a covered dome activated by a lever on the side. Bets are made according to the predicted fall of the dice, the only difference between the two games being in the type of bets on offer.

In the illustrations over the page you can see the odds for each bet in both games. However, be sure to check these figures against those given in the casino's Gaming Guide as the layout and some of the bets may vary from place to place. This is particularly relevant for the group which includes Big and Small. As a matter of course it is better to go for the lower-odds bets because those offering higher returns generally have a higher house margin. This will become clearer in a moment.

Mini Dice

There are two types of bets made with Mini-dice: those on 'Numbers' and those for a 'Field' (see layout). With

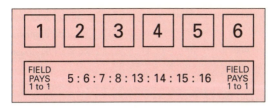

Layout for Mini Dice.

Numbers bets you are asked to select a number from one to six in boxes provided. This is done by placing a stake in the appropriate box. Then it is just a matter of praying that that number will appear at least once when the dice are spun. If one die shows your number, the odds are at even money; if two show your number the odds are 2/1; and for all three the odds are 10/1. Considering that overseas versions of the game return 3/1 for all three numbers it is here that the Australian version makes up some of the difference on the house take, even if the chance of making this throw is 215/1.

Field bet numbers are 5, 6, 7, 8, 13, 14, 15 and 16. Again a bet is marked by placing a stake in the appropriate box only here you are going for the total of the three dice. Odds are at even money but note carefully that the probability of some numbers occurring are far greater than others: those at the beginning and end of the scale are heavily against you. Below is a table showing the probability of each.

4 or 17	70/1
5 or 16	35/1
6 or 15	20.6/1
7 or 14	13.4/1
8 or 13	9.3/1
9 or 12	7.6/1
10 or 11	7/1

Comparing the above mentioned return from Field bets with the probability of even the BEST of these numbers occurring (7/1 for 10 or 11) you can see that the house take here is very high.

Big and Small (also known as Sic Bo or Tai Sai)

As mentioned earlier the only difference between this form of simple dice game and Mini-Dice is in the types of bets offered. This becomes evident when studying the layout below where it can be seen that there are many more combinations of the dice to bet on with a corresponding area on the board for each.

As a guide to the house margins for each of the bets, around 3% is average for the even money wagers and around 7-12% for some of the longer shots.

Layout of a Big and Small table.

TWO-UP

Two-Up has the notable distinction of being the only wholly Australian game played in a casino. What perhaps is even more notable about it though is that despite its long history and its immense popularity with the Australian public it is only in the various casinos around Australia that it has been legalized. The only exception to this is Kalgoorlie, a gold mining town in the outback of Western Australia, where it was legalized in the mid-seventies.

The game is believed to have started in the Victorian goldfields as early as the 1850s. It rose to prominence and spread throughout Australia, particularly in the goldfields and the outback, around the 1890s. By the time of the First World War it had become a national obsession and consequently a part of the ANZAC legend, much to the chagrin of the authorities who were doing their best to discourage the game.

In this climate several Two-Up schools started, each cunningly designed to avoid the strong arm of the law. One of the most famous of these was 'Thommos', founded by Joe Thomas, who conducted one of the notorious 'floating' Two-Up schools. These schools were 'floating' by the dozen at the time, the idea being that should they get a hint of the constabulary approaching they would simply walk (well, perhaps run) away and set up shop somewhere else. The schools were therefore designed to be temporary and the legendary Thommo successfully evaded the authorities for some 60 odd years from 1908 onwards.

The first legal game of Two-Up was played at Wrest Point Casino when it opened in 1973. Now it appears as staple fare at every casino in Australia and maintains its popularity. Perhaps one reason for this is that it somehow captures the Australian spirit since unlike the other casino games which are often hushed and serious, Two-Up is played with much mirth and uses a distinctly Aussie vernacular.

The rules of the game as played in a casino are slightly different from those played elsewhere. Two-Up casino style is played in a ring with a house dealer, called the 'boxer', and a 'spinner' who is selected from amongst the players standing outside the ring. The familiar phrase 'Come in spinner' beckons the next player waiting into the limelight. Once inside the ring he or she is handed a 'kip', a wooden spade-like implement used to toss the two coins.

The spinner's goal is to spin Heads three times without spinning either five consecutive Odds (a head and a tail) or Tails. If he or she succeeds they receive odds of 7.5/1 for their wager and they can continue as spinner. If that

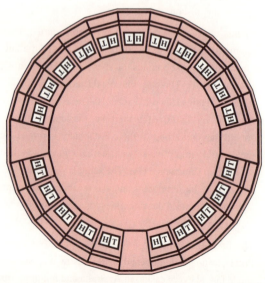

The pit.

TERMS USED IN TWO-UP

Kip wooden implement used to spin the coins

Tails both coins showing tails

Heads both coins showing heads

Odds one coin showing heads, the other tails

Spinner the player holding the Kip

Boxer the person conducting the game

Kiss the sound the two coins make when they touch each other

Stand-off when all bets are frozen until the next throw

Player those betting outside the pit

person fails they retire as spinner and the next person waiting is called. The coins must be tossed at least one metre above head-height. They must also spin. If neither of these happen a 'no game' is called, wagers are frozen (called a 'stand-off'), and the toss is repeated.

Players stand outside the ring and while waiting their turn as spinner are betting on the fall of each toss. The idea is to successfully predict either Heads or Tails for each throw, to win or lose. The odds are even money so if you pick Heads and it comes up you get double your money: your wager plus the same again from the 'bank'. If Tails come up you lose whatever you wagered. Odds are counted as a stand-off unless five consecutive Odds fall in a row in which case the spinner and players all lose. That is, the bank takes all wagers currently on the board. Note that the spinner is also entitled to make even money bets. In Two-Up the house take is around 3%.

Two-Up Renegade Style

Here, as in the casino version, the game is controlled by the boxer who is in charge of selecting the spinner and handling the betting, including any side-betting. Traditionally the boxer is the person running the school — they make their money by taking a 'rake-off' (commission) from the winning bets including, again, any side-bets.

Once all bets are in the spinner throws the coins and as long as there is not a stand-off the matter is simply and uncontroversially decided. Usually the spinner is going for Heads, everyone else for Tails. As long as the spinner can keep throwing Heads they are permitted to keep the kip. Unlike the casino version where that person will be asked to retire after five consecutive stand-offs as well as on a throw of Tails, here it is only the Tails that will lose it for them.

AUSTRALIA'S LONGEST-RUNNING TWO-UP GAME

Apart from being the first Two-Up school to be legalized (in July 1983), the game at Kalgoorlie is also the longest-running, dating back to the 1890s. Originally it 'floated' but later established itself in a rusty sheet-iron enclosure about seven kilometres north of the town. Kalgoorlie itself is an old gold-mining centre 600km east of Perth. Gold is still mined there today.

MACHINE GAMES

POKER MACHINES

Not only are Poker Machines, or the 'Pokies' as they are more commonly and affectionately known, one of the simplest of gambling games they are also one of the most popular. In fact, after horse racing (by far the most popular form of gambling in terms of money spent) they streak ahead of everything else. This is despite the fact that in every state and territory, each of which has its own regulating body, there are considerable restrictions on where the game can be played, outside casinos.

One reason for this is that since their introduction they have been branded with allegations of corruption, apparently a carry-over from the days of prohibition in America when the Mafia were thought to be laundering money through Pokies in place of alcohol. Another reason, one closer to home, is that other gambling institutions have successfully lobbied to keep the machines out. Even NSW, the most liberal of the states concerned, has had a chequered history with Pokies, resulting in Royal Commissions, judgements ruled then overturned and so on.

To some extent this situation is changing. South Australia and Queensland have both passed legislation to allow Poker Machines to operate in those states, and Queensland is developing an on-line/off-line system throughout the state. Even the Victorian government, known for its conservatism, has indicated that it may in the future legislate in favour of Poker Machines. The increasing number of casinos, all of which have Poker Machines available, should also be taken into account.

The various state governments are well advised to pass legislation in favour of Poker Machines for they are good tax payers. The takes on the machines vary a lot, depending on the state concerned and whether it is a hotel, club or casino, but be assured that it is a healthy amount. For example in NSW the state government takes between 3-4% of the takings of hotel-type Poker Machines leaving the hotel concerned (and its supplier) a potential 12% profit. The minimum allowed payout for hotels is 85% of the revenue. So, bearing in mind that other Poker Machines take similar amounts from the incredible quantities of money that are turned over each year, you can begin to understand why NSW League, RSL and sporting clubs look so healthy. In fact $1.25 billion is turned over in the industry every year, $280 million of which is returned in tax revenue.

We shall look at how the machines are programmed for their takes a little later, an understanding of this is important in learning how you can win on the Poker Machines, or rather, why you can't. But first let us look at the two types of games currently played in Australia. Note that casinos usually have both types of machines and hotels in NSW play the Draw Card version.

Club Games

The first 'Pokie' machines go back to the 1880s in America. These were the original 'one-armed bandits' with a lever at one side and the fruit symbols appearing in the window. In this form they were transported to Australia. However Australians soon adopted symbols that more closely represented a Poker hand and later most of the manually operated machines were replaced by the push-button machines we see today.

Games are played with either 5c, 10c, 20c, $1 and $2 coins, 10c machines are the most popular, then 20c machines. Each machine takes only one type of coin but you can play 1-5 coins at a time with a proportional increase in potential winnings with every additional coin played.

Each machine has its own winning combinations of cards, however the top payouts are invariably three, four or five cards of a kind — for example, Kings. Naturally, five Kings will pay more than three. But this is not to say that 5 Jacks, for example, will pay more than three Kings because each symbol (or card or kind) pays out a different amount. One reason for this is that there are more of the lesser-paying cards.

Another variation between machines is that while some play each hand straight across the machine (you can see a line drawn across the screen indicating where the machine is playing), others play straight across the machine for some combinations and in other directions for others. Perhaps it will play across the top of the screen instead, or at adjacent angles, or in an enclosed box.

Playing a game is simply a matter of pushing a button corresponding to how many coins you are willing to chance. The wheels spin, stop and you are automatically credited or debited the amount either won or lost. This is

---

POKER MACHINE MONEY MANAGEMENT

Most people who play Poker machines seem to derive pleasure from losing their money slowly. However if you were betting $100 on the Pokies you would be better off tipping the lot in at once and seeing how you fare. This is because the house profit margin guarantees you will lose that amount of money invested if you play long enough. In a nutshell, the longer you play, the greater your chances of losing. That is how the statistics work. Poker machines don't take $100 bills of course; your best bet, mathematically speaking, is to play five coins at $1 or whatever is the maximum possible.

shown beside 'credit' on the jackpot screen. When your credit is zero you either leave or put some more coins in.

If however you have been lucky enough to win, or at least you still have some credit left when you have finished playing, you push the 'collect' button and the number of coins registered on the credit meter will be returned to you in the tray.

Note though that most machines have a coin limit of 300 coins in the tray. Any number of coins greater than this amount and you are directed to see the attendant who will either pay you cash or write you a cheque. The choice is yours, though if you have won the jackpot or another very large sum of money you may have to take the cheque, for the understandable reason that it is not practical for the venue concerned to keep huge amounts of money on the premises. As far as I know there are no clubs or casinos which really do keep wheelbarrows!

The other button you will see on the machine is 'reserve'. It does exactly this while you are seeing the attendant about credit or up at the bar buying yourself a drink or calling your spouse. You get the idea.

In-house and Cross Linking

This is a variation on the game where a number of machines are linked to each other in a bank all playing for a common jackpot or jackpots. The machines may be linked within a club (In-house Linking) or between clubs (Cross-Linking). The machines are played exactly the same way, however a small percentage of the coins tipped into the slots goes towards a jackpot pool. The current total of this pool is usually displayed on digital screens above the banks as well as on the machines themselves. The appeal of the game is in watching the jackpots increase while you are playing and of course the great amounts of money that can be won. One or two smaller jackpots may be paid out for other less rare combinations. At present a $100,000 jackpot limit is set for these machines with any increment flowing over into the next jackpot.

Draw card

Like the other form of Poker Machine in this game you have the choice of playing one to five coins at a time. There are also five cards in any one play, each 'dealt' to you by way of a random number generator. This game is based directly on the standard Draw form of Poker and though there are some variations between the machines they are all more or less as described here. The differences between this game and the casino version are as follows.

The symbols used all strictly adhere to a conventional pack of cards: you are dealt a hand exactly as though it were a Poker hand. You also complete the play in the same fashion, by holding the cards you want to keep and drawing from a pack for the rest. After drawing once (you can of course keep your first hand) the machine will either give you credit if you have won or take away the value of your play if you haven't. You have won if your hand contains at least two pairs. Any higher scoring hand wins you increasingly greater amounts of credit. See the chapter on Poker in this book if you are unsure what winning Poker hands look like. Here you will also find the odds of drawing a particular hand.

If you have won a hand the machine then gives you the opportunity to double your existing credit, or lose the lot. Alternatively you can 'half gamble' which means you only lose half your existing credit if you lose, or win one and a half times your existing credit if you win.

This part is played by selecting either a 'red' or a 'black' draw on your winning hand. The machine asks you which you would prefer, you choose and the machine takes the other. A colour is then selected at random by the program. Odds are even at this stage and luck determines who will come up the winner. You can play this as many times as you like or until you have no credit left. Unfortunately the latter is very frequent unless you are blessed with restraint or amazing good fortune.

The buttons on the machine are fairly self explanatory. 'Bet 1', 'Bet 2' etc. refer to how many coins you are prepared to play. The buttons below allow you to hold cards. Then there are the 'draw', 'gamble', 'half gamble', 'hold' 'red', 'black' and 'collect' buttons. They do exactly what they say.

How the Machines are Programmed

Although the mathematics behind Poker Machines are quite complicated, the fundamentals are simple enough to understand, once explained, and worth going through if only to understand why your pockets are emptying rather than filling. Also, as a mathematical exercise it is quite intriguing.

First of all the machines are not 'fixed' in the sense that the wheels spin in conjunction with others or are somehow calculated to land in a certain sequence. This would make things too easy for dedicated Pokie-busters to crack the combinations. The wheels do indeed spin at random, the manufacturers make sure of it, and the takes work as follows.

For the purposes of this exercise and to keep the calculations relatively simple let's take a fictional Pokie Machine with a five card hand, each of which is on a reel of six cards. Assume also that the six cards are K, Q, J, 10, 9 and 8 although in practice this is not the case.

You have inserted a coin and now the reels spin. You

can see that for each reel there is a one in six chance of a particular card occurring. Say it is the King. There is also a one in six chance of the King occurring on the next reel, and so on. Therefore the probability of the King occurring on all five reels is 1/6 x 1/6 x 1/6 x 1/6 x 1/6 or one in 7776 chances.

Five Kings wins the jackpot. But there are other prizes: two Kings perhaps. The possibility of this is 1/6 x 1/6 or one in 36 chances. The same can be calculated for any combination of cards. Each machine has its own combinations of cards which pay out.

Now the programmer behind the machine knows that they want to pay out 90% of the takings to the punter and keep 10% in the machine for tax and revenue. Assuming that the punter is playing with $1 coins the programmer knows that for every $7776 poured into the machine there is one chance of someone scoring the jackpot and let's say eight chances of another combination occurring, 24 chances of another and so on for all the combinations the machine is paying on. Since 90% of $7776 is $6994.80, which is what the programmer wants to pay, they distribute that sum across the range of combinations, obviously paying out more for those combinations which are the most infrequent.

This is not to say that there will ALWAYS be a jackpot for every 7776 coins tipped in, or that there will ALWAYS be 24 payouts of another combination, but taken over an extended period it will come very close to it. In other words the programmer is making a sure bet.

The type of game described here roughly corresponds to the Poker Machines that are played in clubs and casinos. Hotel Pokies work on the same principle although the method of playing them is slightly different.

The implication of all this number-crunching is that just as the casino or club can be sure of making money over a period of plays so the punter can be sure of losing it. Unlike some other gambling games there is no degree of 'knowledge' involved in playing the Pokies so you are playing directly against the system which, I repeat, is unbeatable over a period of time. This is the reason why serious gamblers avoid the Pokies like the plague. If you are fortunate enough to win some money, keep it. Don't tempt fate. Otherwise treat the game as an amusement and don't be surprised or disappointed if you are down at the end of the day.

Against this advice there are some machines which are thought to have better odds than others or, in other words, take less. I would place my bets on machines which are near the entrance of a venue. The idea is, of course, that they will be attempting to draw people in by virtue of a few prominent satisfied customers. Maybe!

One other thing to bear in mind is that hotel and club Poker Machines are generally programmed to pay out less than those in casinos. Since the amount to be paid out is governed by law, the table below which shows the minimum payouts required from casinos may be of interest. At the time of publication NSW, Victoria and the ACT do not have casinos. The minimum payout required of NSW clubs is 85% and of ACT clubs, 88%.

Northern Territory	88%
Queensland	92%
Western Australia	92%
South Australia	92%
Tasmania	90%

Note that these are the MINIMUM payouts. The venues concerned are entitled to pay more and usually do to keep punters interested. A figure of around 89% for clubs would be average.

KENO

Keno is a relatively new game to Australia but is rapidly becoming one of the favourite forms of coupon betting. Every Australian casino offers Keno and several states are now offering it as part of their lotteries group. In essence it is very much like Bingo and Lotto, with coloured balls drawn from a barrel called a 'goose'. It is therefore a game of chance only, offering at best large payouts for very small sums of money, but against incredible odds. There are however many smaller prizes in Keno.

In this part of the book I will be looking at Keno as it is played in casinos, however there is in effect little difference between this version and that offered by the various lottery groups so that what applies to one equally applies to the others.

The main advantages of Keno are that it is quick, easy and large numbers of people can play it at any one time. For this reason it has a high profile in the casino with staff (called 'Keno Runners') and screens appearing throughout the establishments. The idea is that anyone, regardless of what else they are doing, can play the game. A new Keno game starts every few minutes throughout the day.

There are two types of bets on Keno: 'Straight' betting and 'Way' betting. Straight betting is the easiest of the two so I shall explain the fundamentals of the game using this as an illustration. How to make Way bets will be explained further on.

Straight Betting

Each game is played with 20 numbers picked at random from 80 coloured ping-pong type balls bouncing into slots from a transparent container. By this stage all players' cards have been validated at the terminals much the same as with Lotto.

The cards themselves allow the punter to select from one to fifteen numbers in any order. The player may then choose the amount he or she is prepared to wager (anywhere from $1 to $9999) and the number of games they wish to play with the one card. A player may also have the opportunity to go for a jackpot as explained later.

Say you select one number, meaning you have placed one 'x' on the card of 80 boxes. This means you have a one in four chance of winning a prize. (Remember there are 20 numbers chosen from 80 in the barrel.) If you pick five numbers you are betting that of the twenty numbers drawn you will have picked five. The chances

An Entry card.

of this are slimmer so the payout rate is increased. What's more, you will still receive prizes if only three or four of the five numbers you have selected are drawn. In all cases the prizes are apportioned according to the risk you are prepared to take. All prizes are advertised in brochures put out by the various casinos with some slight differences in the payout rates. Similarly, the payout rates of the lottery versions differ. The most popular bet is the 10 number ticket, which pays upwards of five numbers drawn from the ten selected. With a $1 bet you can win $25 000 if all of your ten numbers are drawn. If five are drawn you win $2.

Way Betting

The rules for Way betting are the same as for Straight betting except that with the former you can combine two or more bets on the one ticket. For example, on the ticket in the diagram below you will see two groups of three crosses circled. Taking the crosses in the top circle first, consider this as the equivalent of playing three Straight numbers on the one game. The same goes for the bottom three. Then consider that all six numbers circled on the ticket constitute a game of Straight numbers as well so that in effect you are playing three

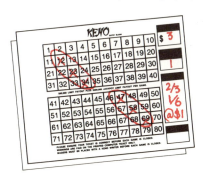

An example of Way betting.

More ideas for Way betting.

different games on the one ticket. For this you pay three times the price: Way tickets are designed as a variation on Straight tickets, to make things a little more interesting. The payouts are the same as for Straight betting.

The number of 'ways' you can play this particular game are almost endless and entirely up to you. You don't have to play all the combinations available on the one ticket either. The set of symbols you see on the side of the ticket that looks suspiciously like school fractions is in fact your selection of combinations. If for instance you wanted to play only the two groups of three numbers on the previous example (that is, you didn't want to play all six numbers together) you would write 2/3 only on the side.

An alternative to this is to select from a range of Way

combinations given by the casino. In this case you simply select which Way you wish to play and pick your lucky numbers. Note that once again you can select how many combinations you wish to play. See illustrations.

Jackpots

If you are playing five or more numbers on the one ticket and you are prepared to make a minimum bet of $2 then you can play for the jackpot. All that is required is to tick the box so marked. Jackpots are won when all your numbers are drawn and the value of the jackpot depends in part on what the current total of the jackpot is, in part how many other winners there are and in part how many numbers you played — the more numbers,

Yet more ideas for Way betting.

the bigger your share of the prizewinnings. Contributions towards the jackpot are made whenever the jackpot box is ticked and the extent of the contributions is the determining factor to how much can be won.

On the subject of maximum limits note that the payout limit for each Keno game is $50 000. In other words the casino will pay out prizes to the value of $50 000 only, no more. If the total claim to the prizes exceeds that amount, the $50 000 allowed is distributed to the prizewinners claiming $200 ($100 in some places) or more in proportion to their win and the number of players involved. This maximum does not apply to jackpots, nor to the lotteries version of the game.

As mentioned earlier, Keno can be played from just about anywhere in the casino. Staff are easy to recognize — just look for the sign saying 'Keno' emblazoned across their clothing somewhere. Alternatively look for the terminals which are situated at regular intervals around the building.

Frankly, the odds of winning a substantial prize at Keno are relatively poor and the casino take is quite high (if 2/1 is given on one number drawn, when there is a 3/1 chance of it appearing, then the casino is taking 25%), but if you enjoy it, why not?

RACING

John Smith
Bookmaker

BETTING WITH THE BOOKIES

There are three main codes involved in the racing game: the gallops and the trots (horses, known as thoroughbreds and standardbreds), and the dogs (greyhounds). The rules are similar in all three, as are the methods of gambling on them. For the purposes of this section of The Australian Gambler's Guide we shall examine the most popular code, the gallops.

Punting on horse racing takes place right across the country from the wide open spaces of Flemington and Randwick, where the accent is on glamour and riches, to the annual picnic meetings in the outback, where dust hangs in the air and the horses go around for a few dollars in prize money. Surprisingly the racing industry is the third largest earner of revenue for Australia's state and federal governments. It employs many thousands of people and turns over billions of dollars, and these are the dollars of a vast army of punters.

But first let us take a look at the basics of gambling on the horses, specifically how to bet with bookmakers and how to read and digest the newspaper formguides.

There are two elementary differences between betting with a bookmaker and betting at the TAB: with the bookmaker you are pitting your skill against a gambler who sets out to operate their 'book' so that they will show a profit regardless of which horse wins the race. This works in theory but certainly not always in practice, although bookmakers are never seen around town in broken down Holdens. The most important difference is that when you place your bet with the bookmaker you take the price they have on offer at that time for the horse you fancy. Those odds and other details about the wager are entered into the bookmaker's official betting sheets and nothing can alter them. When you bet with the TAB you do so through a computer, and the odds you receive will not be determined until the moment the starter presses the button to send the runners on their journey. Then all betting ceases, and you will know only approximately what you stand to win.

How to place a bet

You are at the races, and the bookmakers are calling the odds. There are usually three people in each bookmaking team: the (boss) bookmaker, who takes the wager and writes the ticket; a bagman, who operates the bookmaker's big white bag (containing money); and the clerk, who writes the details of every bet into an official sheet. When you are due to collect from the bookmaker you present your ticket and the details will be called out to the clerk, who will check them against his sheet and verify the amount due to you.

The bookmaker operates a 'book' on each race. Through their clerk's figures they are able to ascertain in a moment the state of the book, for instance how much they have laid against each horse and where they will stand, balance-wise, if horse such-and-such or horse so-and-so wins the event. The odds that the bookmaker is offering on each runner are quoted on their board, and as the bets are coming in before each race they are making adjustments to the board, either lengthening or shortening the odds about the runners according to the bets being made. On the following page is an imaginary market on a board.

The bookmaker is saying that if you put $1 on Slattery's Nosh to win (also known as a 'straight-out' bet) and the horse does win, the bagman will hand you back $5, representing the four he bet you plus the dollar you laid

Slattery's Nosh	4
Nifty Boy	2
Kooka Kottage	8
Jacqui's Dilemma	5/2
Noisy Joan	5
Redd William	20
Lily Shoes	16
Braybrook	20

out. If you wish to have $1 each way on Slattery's Nosh, and he wins, you will receive $7 back in the hand, representing your stake ($2), plus the four for the win and $1 for the place. It is important to understand this, for 4/1 is a key to betting with bookmakers. It is the 'money back' bet for place-only betters. We have seen that your $1 for the place on Slattery's Nosh brought you a profit of $1, which is a quarter of the 4/1 *each-way* price on the horse which you accepted from the bookmakers. The 'money back' situation works like this: if you put $1 each way on Slattery's Nosh and he finishes second, or third, you will receive $2 from the bagman. You lost your $1 to win but you received back the $1 you outlaid for the horse to finish in a place PLUS one quarter of the odds, which was another $1. So you outlaid $2 and received that sum back. This is considered to be a sensible way to bet because your horse only had to win or run second or third, and you are 'still in business'. Many punters operate on an *each-way* basis, usually selecting the second or third favourite. To re-cap, if Slattery's Nosh had been at 8/1 in the market and you laid $1 each way and he won, then your collect would be $12, representing the return of your stake ($2) plus the $8 price on the horse AND $2 for the place, again representing a quarter of the 8/1 price. You will always receive one quarter of the odds when you successfully bet for the place with bookmakers.

Moving along, check the imaginary market above once again and you will see that at 4/1, Slattery's Nosh is the third favourite in the field, as far as this particular bookmaker is concerned at this point in the betting. Remember that the bookmaker offers prices on the runners depending on the weight of money coming in for each horse. This, basically, is how they operate. They will sometimes take risks, but will always be attempting to work themselves into a no-loss situation. The favourite horse is Nifty Boy, at twos (2/1). It is hardly worthwhile backing him for a place, because his odds are short. If you put $20 on him straight out ('on the nose'), and he does win, the bookmaker's clerk will hand you $60 — your $20 (outlay) and their $40, representing $20 at 2/1.

The second favourite is Jacqui's Dilemma, at 5/2. This actually equates to the simple fraction 2.5/1, slightly longer odds than the outright favourite, Nifty Boy, at 2/1. If you put $1 on Jacqui's Dilemma straight-out, and she wins, you will receive $3.50 in hand, representing your $1 outlay plus the bookmaker's $2.50. If you put $200 on her, the bagman will hand you $700 (their five and your two). It should go without saying that if these horses do not win, you may have to walk home.

Remember that once you take the price on the board there is no retreat, and that nothing, not even an earthquake, can alter it. If you take the fours on Slattery's Nosh and it 'blows' to sixes, you've got the fours and are stuck with them. If on the other hand there is a big move for Slattery's Nosh and it finally starts at say threes, then you have taken a more generous price. Experience will teach you when to move in for your bets.

Sometimes the odds shown on a bookmaker's board

appear complicated, but really they are logical and present no problems after your initial study. You need to remember that a horse can start 'in the red' or 'in the black.' 'In the red' means that a horse is at odds-on, a situation which arises only when a horse is a red-hot favourite and is considered a certainty to win the race. Odds-on is simply this: you will recall that Nifty Boy was our phantom favourite at 2/1. This meant 2/1 'against'. In other words, if you put $1 on him to win, and he did win, you would receive $3 back — your dollar plus the bookmaker's two dollars (2/1). Had Nifty Boy been quoted at 2/1-on (odds-on) then you would have risked your $2 to gain a profit of the bookmaker's $1. In another example, if you put $100 on Nifty Boy at the odds of 2/1-on and he won, you would be handed $150, representing your outlay ($100) plus the book-

THE START OF HORSE RACING

Horse racing was introduced into Australia soon after the early settlers arrived and grew in popularity until almost every town of a thousand people or more boasted its own track. It was in October 1810 however that the first legal race was conducted, under Governor Macquarie's custodianship. This was at Hyde Park, in Sydney, and Governor Macquarie's orders that no gaming, drunkenness, swearing, quarrelling, fighting or boxing was to be tolerated was resoundingly ignored as Sydney celebrated the event for three straight days. Here, as later in Queensland, the race was run clockwise while in all other states to this day they are raced anti-clockwise.

maker's $50. But remember that the bookie only stood to lose $50 while you stood to lose $100 had Nifty Boy been beaten.

We turn now to the table below which explains the fractions of odds used by most bookmakers. (In South Australia the odds are down to even closer fractions). Observe that the odds-on and odds-against figures are split by the word 'evens'. This means that if Nifty Boy was at evens and you put $1 (to win) on him and he won, you would receive back from the bagman $2, representing your dollar and the bookie's (even) dollar:

> **Odds-on**
> The profit you stand to make is *less* than the amount you risk
> 1/4, 2/7, 1/3, 2/5, 4/9, 1/2, 4/7, 8/13, 4/6, 8/11, 4/5, 9/10.
>
> **Evens**
> Sometimes referred to as even money
>
> **Odds-against**
> The potential profit is *greater* than the sum you risk
> 10/9, 5/4, 11/8, 6/4, 13/8, 7/4, 2/1, 9/4, 5/2, 11/4, 3/1, and so on.

Just remember that fractional odds of 7/2 mean 3.5/1. These margins are important, so it pays to become familiar with them. Some punters will back odds-on chances; others will scorn them and not bet in the race because of the risks involved plus the need to outlay a lot of money in order to win a little. A champion horse of the late 1930s, Ajax, once started at 40/1-on at Rosehill. This meant the punters had to risk £40 as the money was then in order to show a profit of one pound

A sample Bookmaker's board.

if Ajax won. He didn't. He was taken to the cleaners. Lest we forget.

How to understand formguides

The daily newspapers provide all the details the punter needs in order to study the form and make selections. The format for metropolitan (city) and provincial meetings is fairly uniform throughout Australia. The front page of the guide usually contains the fields, plus many other pieces of intelligence, and the detailed form (previous runs) of each horse is printed over the page. First, let us examine the front page of a phantom formguide to discover what all the figures are about.

The front page of the guide tells you at a glance what you need to know. It details the numbers, names and times for each race on the card, as well as the class of the event, and the names of every runner. It gives the tipsters' selections. It tells you what races are being used for daily doubles, quadrellas and so on. It supplies a legend which you can match with the form of each runner. It provides an overnight (approximate) market to give an assessment of how the betting on raceday is expected to shape up. The best way to understand the legend, an important service when the punter is searching for a winner, is to use our phantom formguide below.

1	123	Slattery's Nosh 1 (tw)...	V. Price	57
2	1202	Nifty Boy 6 (t)...	J. Palance	56
3	56004	Kooka Kottage 5...	E. Robinson	54.5
4	10s43	Jacqui's Dilemma 7 (cwd)	P. Cushing	54.5
5	0432	Noisy Joan 3...	T. Savalas	54
6	04p4	Redd William...	H. Silva	54
7	3f07	Lily Shoes 8...	C. Lee	53.5
8	200x	Braybrook 4...	I. Amin	53

Here is the legend —

t: *the horse has won on this course.*

w: *the horse has won on a wet track.*

d: *the horse has won over the distance of its race, but at some other course.*

c: *the horse has won on this course and at this distance.*

x: *the horse lost its rider.*

s: *the horse resumed after having a spell.*

*: *the horse started favourite at its last start.*

p: *the horse was pulled up.*

f: *the horse fell.*

Now match the legend and the details for each horse in our phantom field. Slattery's Nosh is officially number 1 (called the 'topweight'). The 3 next to his name means he finished third at his most recent run, the 2 means he finished second at the previous run and the 1 means he won the race before that. There are only three digits next to his name because he has had only three career runs. The 1 after his name means he has drawn gate number 1 at the starting stalls. The *tw* means (check legend) he has previously won on this course and in the wet (meaning a rain-affected course). His jockey is V. Price, and the weight (handicap) he must carry is 57 kilograms.

Now check inside the formguide, where you will find many more details about each horse including personal statistics such as its breeding, its age, its trainer, and how much money it has won in stakes. Then there will be facts relevant to its previous few runs, such as where it finished, the venue, the date, the state of the track, what weight it carried, the jockey, the margins between the placed horses, the time the race took, the track conditions, the number of runners in the race, the class of the race, and so on.

PLACING A BET WITH THE TAB

Most betting at the TAB is on horse racing and the general background of selecting a horse and placing a bet has already been covered in the preceding section on betting with the bookies.

However, the TAB (or Totalisator Agency Board to give it the full title) provides opportunities to gamble on many other sporting events besides horse racing. It also makes gambling very easy by providing shops and agencies where punters can lay their bets. Wherever you live in Australia, providing it is in an urban area, you will never be far from a TAB.

In recent years these government owned bodies have expanded their services to cover not only horse racing, the trots and the dogs, but also football (Rugby League or Australian Rules, depending on the state) and special events such as the Sydney to Hobart yacht race and the motor racing Grand Prix in Adelaide. For example, in Western Australia where Australian Rules is played a bet is offered where you may enter a game where you pick the winning team plus the winning margin (within brackets of ten points). Most of the other states likewise offer two or three types of entry for each round of football. Like betting on the races, the prize pool is made up from the punters' revenue and is distributed evenly across the range of winners. Tickets are simple to fill out but your local TAB shop will also have brochures to help you understand the rules.

Now to the races. Because the format of the betting tickets varies slightly between states, and is subject to ongoing changes designed to make betting easier for the customers, we will explain the procedures in general.

There is no mystery involved, in fact the TAB continue to make wagering simpler as their computer systems become ever more sophisticated. Inside the agency you will find pens and entry slips for all manner of bets and easy instructions on how to mark your slip in order to make a wager.

There are many different types of bets available, as follows: betting for the win; betting for the place; betting each way; quinellas; running doubles; trifectas; superfectas (NSW only); quadrellas; quadXtras; daily doubles; extra doubles. Brief explanations follow.

Betting for the Win

This is called betting 'on the nose'. Imagine that you fancy a horse named Slattery's Nosh in the first race at Flemington. He is horse number 1 in race 1. Fifty-cent units are used in Victoria (the denomination varies from state to state) and you wish to put $1 on Slattery's Nosh (to win). You enter the TAB shop and pick up a 'win and place' slip. You now mark the slip with strokes of the pen in the squares provided, so that the completed slip records the information that the bet is on the races (as opposed to trots and/or greyhounds); that the venue is a city track, in this case Flemington; that your wager is in race 1; that the official number of the horse is 1; and that you are wagering two units on Slattery's Nosh to win the race, as opposed to running second or third.

You then feed your marked slip into a computer manned by a window operator, hand over your money and wait. The computer processes and records the details of the wager, and the operator hands back to you the ticket imprinted with the relevant details. If Slattery's Nosh does not win, you have lost your money. Remember that it matters not if he runs second or third, because you backed him to win the race.

Betting for the Place

As above, except that you have backed Slattery's Nosh to finish in a place, i.e. first, second or third. This will become clearer in a moment. The only change on the slip you prepare is that you mark the section for the horse to run a place (as opposed to winning outright). Understand that if Slattery's Nosh wins the race you still receive only what he pays for the place. Same if he runs second, same if he runs third. This becomes clearer as follows:

Betting Each Way

The formula for making the each-way bet remains the same except that you are backing Slattery's Nosh to win the race and also to finish in a place. Thus, if you wish to place say $1 each way on him then you enter these details on the betting slip. This means you are wagering $1 that Slattery's Nosh wins the race and a *further* $1 that he is placed (first, second or third). If he wins, then you receive back (from the window operator) whatever price he pays for that $1 you invested on him to win. Say he pays $3 for the win. For this investment you will receive $4. You have also invested on him for the place. Say he pays $1 for the place. For this investment you will receive $2. Summed up, you have invested two units each way (a $2 outlay) and received in the hand $6 after Slattery's Nosh wins the race. If he runs second or third, you will lose the two units you wagered on him for the win but still receive his place price, totalling $2 and meaning that you finish square on the deal, you get your outlay back. If Slattery's Nosh fails to run first, second or third, you lose all of your outlay.

Quinella

You must back the horses that finish first and second in the race of your choice. Let us say that you fancy number

> ### THE GREAT PHAR LAP
>
> Everyone has heard of the horse Phar Lap. A New Zealand bred chestnut gelding, he won 37 races from 51 starts including, in 1930, the Melbourne Cup. In 1932 he was taken to the US where four days after his first start (which he won) he was found dead. Some accused the Mafia of killing him,, but the real reason has never been found. Today his stuffed and mounted body is on display at the State Museum of Victoria while his heart, the largest ever found in a horse, is preserved at the National Museum in Canberra. He stood 17.5 hands high (a 'hand' is 4 inches and is measured to the shoulder of the horse).

1, Slattery's Nosh, and number 3, Nifty Boy, to take out the quinella for the event in which they are running. You fill out a special slip for quinellas in the usual way (and if you have bother with this you can always seek assistance from a fellow punter) nominating numbers 1 and 3 to take the quinella. You have backed the winning quinella regardless of whether Slattery's Nosh or Nifty Boy wins, so long as the other runs second. In other words, the winning quinella can be 1 and 3 or 3 and 1.

Running Doubles

In this form of betting you are trying to couple the winners of two races on the program. Let's say that Slattery's Nosh is in race 4 and Nifty Boy is in race 5. You fancy them both to win their races so you fill in the betting slip accordingly. Both must win, and of course if they do oblige then the odds will usually be much more attractive than for straight-out bets on both. (All this depends upon how fancied they are in the market, see the section on Betting with the Bookmakers.)

Trifectas

Same as for quinellas, basically, except that you must nominate the first three placegetters instead of just the winner and the second horse. You can have a lot of fun with these more exotic forms of wagering, and you can return handsome profits if you are lucky. But, as someone once remarked, it ain't easy.

Superfectas

These are available in NSW, and to snare one you will need a brave heart and luck on your side. You have to nominate the first six horses across the line. Say no more.

Quadrellas

These are hugely popular. You have to nominate the winners of four selected events on the card. It is difficult, to say the least, but big profits can be made.

QuadXtras

The same as above except that the races chosen are slightly different to those of the quadrella.

Daily Doubles

Here you have to nominate the winners of two chosen races, often the feature events on the program.

Extra Doubles

These are similar except that they are operated on two different races.

OTHER RACES

What has been discussed in the previous section concerning betting on horse races also applies to several other types of races held throughout Australia, the greyhounds and trots of course, but also such events as the Great Camel Race in Alice Springs, the Stawell Gift (a footrace) in Victoria and the spectacular eighteen-footers on Sydney Harbour. On all of these gambling is legal, either through a licensed bookmaker or maybe through the TAB. In this section we'll look briefly at some of these races. Just follow the advice given for thoroughbreds if you wish to place a bet.

A word on the licensing of bookmakers. A 'licensed' bookmaker is one who is registered with a state racing control body. The idea of licences was introduced to stamp out fraudulent operators who thrived in the industry in the early days of racing. The word 'dodgy' was used literally since if bookmakers found themselves in trouble for any reason (for example, they had no money to pay punters their winnings!) they would simply disappear. Registration thus ensured that punters and the authorities alike knew who they were dealing with, and more importantly, where they could be found since it was a condition of registration that the bookies be 'on the rails', meaning they could be found at the race when it was on. Registration also ensured that the authorities could keep an eye on any duties that might be owed them. Victoria was the first state government to introduce registration of bookmakers in 1882.

Today there are still plenty of illegal bookmakers around, operating off-course. They are known as 'SP' or 'Starting Price' bookies because the odds paid are, like the TAB, the final or starting price' odds. For the reasons given above they are best avoided. This is especially true when betting is over the phone and the SP bookie has a chance to elope with your winnings. Despite all this, the SP bookies are thought to turn over huge sums of money.

The Stawell Easter Gift

This race is run every Easter over two days, finishing with the Grand Final on Easter Monday. Several preliminary races are held to determine who is eligible for the final. The distance of the race is 100 metres.

Stawell itself is an old goldmining town 233km northwest of Melbourne, near the Grampian Range. Although it still has a commercial goldmining industry it is better known now as a farming centre, with the Great Western vineyards just to the south-east. Once boasting a population of 30 000 it has now shrunk to just over 6000. The Stawell Gift was first run in 1878.

The Eighteen Foot Skiffs — Sydney Harbour

Unlike the dozens of other classes of yachts sailing on Australia's waters, the 18 foot skiff, like its younger siblings the 16 foot skiff and the 12 foot skiff, is virtually unrestricted apart from its length. There is no maximum sail area, no restriction on the materials that go into making the boat and no restrictions on sponsorship. No other class of yacht in the world is quite like it: even the America's Cup boats have very strict regulations. Eighteen footers are unique to Australia.

In short, this freedom is the recipe for the colour and excitement that have become their trademark. The huge spinnakers, usually found on boats three of four times their size, the speeds they fly around the course and the corporate logos on the sails are all part of the tradition. So too are the ferries which follow them around the harbour and it is here that most of the gambling takes place, via bookies who lengthen and shorten the odds on the different boats as the race progresses. These sessions can be lively and boozy and if it was not bad enough that several kegs of beer attend a ferry during a race there are stories that in the early days of the sport a keg would often be put on board some of the skiffs as well!

Camel Racing — Alice Springs

Camels were used from the 1860s until the 1920s to carry mining goods, poles for the Overland Telegraph and wool and equipment to and from outback stations. They played an important role in opening up the inland of Australia. When other forms of transport were introduced the camels were set free and multiplied in the wild. Once a year a camel race is held in Alice Springs and bookies will take your money.

Iron Man Event — Wollongong

Surf life saving carnivals have been around for most of this century and are now an Australian institution. The Iron Man contest, which combines surf-swimming, surf-skiing and surfing in the one event, is a relative newcomer to the scene however, being introduced in Sydney in the 1966-67 season. Since then it has quickly became popular and now boasts a Grand Prix circuit attracting sponsorship from major Australian companies. The Wollongong event is part of this circuit and allows betting.

Greyhound Racing

The first greyhound racing was known as 'coursing' which involved two greyhounds in pursuit of a live hare. Later the live hare was replaced by a mechanical one and the open field became an enclosed track. It is in this form that all greyhound racing is run today. Greyhound racing began in NSW in 1927, but was subsequently found to be illegal and closed down. It started again in NSW in the early thirties and other states followed soon after, with rural areas particularly attracted to the sport. Race meetings are frequent and mostly held in the evenings with bookies in attendance. After some initial success greyhound racing is somewhat in decline.

Trotting and Pacing

Trotting and pacing are yoked together under the one name 'trotting' or the 'trots'. They are very similar, the same breed of horse is used (the standardbred), and they share much the same history, but there are nevertheless important differences. The first of these involves the type of gait allowed. With pacers the horse's gait is restricted so that its two side legs move forward at the same time in a rocking, lateral movement. With trotters the gait is restricted diagonally so that the front and hind legs on different sides move forward at the same time. Of the two, pacing is now the more popular, gradually taking over from trots during more than a century of the sport in Australia. There are various reasons offered for this, one being that the smaller tracks in Australia are better suited to pacers, another that the pacers are considered cheaper and easier to train. Of the two however, trotting is more popular worldwide.

Trotting, like greyhounds, is another sport which found popularity after night meetings were legitimized, meaning that both night meetings and betting at them were permitted. It is no coincidence therefore that the first successful trotting track, at Wayville in South Australia, was also the first to allow legitimate night racing. No other state permitted night trotting until after the WWII. Most meetings have on course TAB and bookies at the rails.

AN A-Z GUIDE FOR THE PUNTER

Attack the formguide. Resolve to speculate for a time on either a straight-out, each-way or place basis, or whether you should stick to doubles and quinellas, and so forth. Stick to that decision. Concentrate on one form of punting, then try another until you find your own key.

Be aware of the class system. Watch for horses who perform reasonably when racing above their class. Take heed, then be on the ball when they go around in their true company.

Consider the in-form trainers and riders in the same way that you are attracted to in-form horses.

Don't look for excuses. If a horse you are following keeps grinding away and running distant placings, start after start, then it has probably reached the limit in that class. Most horses cannot win a maiden, even fewer can win at Class 1 and so on.

Educated money (a term indicating that a surge of cash has been wagered on a certain runner) can be worth following, so watch the betting at the track and on the TAB monitors, particularly when a runner from a strong stable keeps firming (in the market). But also bear in mind that a drifter in the market (where the odds keep lengthening) sometimes does win.

Following a successful stable or a leading jockey is a so-so method of punting, mainly because the stable has many runners and the jockey has many mounts. If you must use such a system, do so when the horses involved are short priced.

Get into the habit of watching runners in the mounting yard. Look for muscle, brightness of coat and general contentment. This takes practice and dedication.

Homework is more important than washing your ears. There are no short-cuts. Bookies study the form. So must the punter.

Initiative is called for on rain-affected tracks, and this provides another good reason for attending the races. There are days when a pattern of racing is established early, such as when horses drawn wide (start from a barrier on the outside) are badly disadvantaged.

Jumping horses should not be ignored. Sure, they have to negotiate the obstacles, but once they have demonstrated their fitness and ability they can be just as reliable as flat runners.

Keep your eyes on the papers. See if the horse you backed missed the start or suffered interference, or was blocked for a run. Take note of horses who prove they can carry weight, and of horses with a record of consistency when they strike form.

Lazy punters and dreamers provide big houses and fast cars for bookmakers. You cannot spend five minutes on a formguide and stab a winner unless you are extremely lucky.

Maiden races (where none of the runners has previously won a race) are scorned by most professional punters, and for obvious reasons. Treat with caution. Better, give them a miss. Ditto for races restricted to mares.

Never take strong drink before going to the track, for you may be tempted to punt more than you can afford.

Odds-on, look on. Too risky.

Patience is a keynote. No one backs every winner every day. Wait for the right races. Don't ask other people what they fancy. Take note of the newspaper tipsters, but blindly following them can prove costly.

Question whether the favourite is true or false. Horses

are often backed into favouritism through sentiment, or because they are ridden by a top jockey or prepared by the leading trainer. Decide what you believe should be the top chance, on form, and work on that basis.

Resolve to attend the races rather than always working from the TAB shops. The real punters lurk at the track. Rub shoulders with them. Watch them watching the prices. Buy them a beer. Make them your friend.

Saddlecloths 1, 2 and 3 win a high percentage of races. In handicaps they have earned the right to their ratings because, basically, they are better performed than the others. Bear this in mind.

Take note of racecourse 'mail' but don't follow it blindly. There is nothing worse than making your own choice and then backing another horse because you've been told it is a 'sure thing', only to see your fancy win the race.

Use logic. Favourites win most of the gallops. Concentrate on them, not the 'bolters' (runners at long prices). Far better to back a 2/1 winner than a 100/1 snail.

Value betting is the go. Put your cash back in your pocket if you honestly believe that your fancy is at 'unders' with the bookies. In connection with this, keep checking the tote prices and fluctuations in order to find the best value.

Weak punters bet in every race and leave the track on public transport. Space your bets. Be more selective and maybe take a limousine.

X marks the spot, at the hip pocket, where bookmakers feel pain. Remember, always, that bookmakers are the enemy. They are there to make money. Your money. Feel no pity for them. They are almost human and they can be beaten.

Young horses are generally more reliable than older

horses. Find them, especially in events for two-year olds, put them in the black book and follow them.

Zeal in studying the fine print is a must. Read and digest the stewards' reports. Check the form of every runner before wiping the no-hopers. Make a list of horses who win on wet tracks and another for those who have won first-up (their first run after a spell). Luck is one thing. Accomplishing the mission is another.

Conclusion

The above list only covers the basics. Punters at the tracks are rather like fishermen and gardeners: they will help you sort out any problems associated with understanding the formguide or other aspects which may puzzle you. Just approach one and ask. And good punting!

LOTTERIES

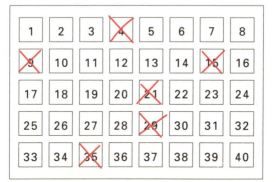

LOTTERIES

The history of lotteries in Australia is in fact the story of Tattersall's, which in turn, is the story of its founder, George Adams who arrived in Australia in 1855 at the age of sixteen. After a spell on the land Adams moved to Sydney and purchased a hotel called O'Brien's. This hotel happened to be the Australian headquarters of the then famous Tattersall's subscription and betting club of London. Here George Adams operated small sweepstakes for his patrons until, with a first prize of £2000, he went public. At this point his troubles began. All forms of gambling were outlawed at the time and despite Adam's reputation for being a fair and honest businessman he attracted much opposition, in particular from the church. Consequently he was forced to move to Queensland where the whole furore started again until finally in 1895, he packed his bags and headed for Tasmania.

It was here that Australians first participated in legitimate lotteries, but not before another type of sweep had been conducted, this time for the assets of the failed Bank of Van Diemen's Land. It was this sweep, administered by Adams, that precipitated the legalization of lotteries. To distribute the bank's assets, Adams issued 100 000 tickets at £1 each for a first prize of a prime piece of real estate in Hobart. The second prize won the ticket holder a pub and the third prize won the bank's building in Launceston. In all some 200 hundred pieces of real estate were distributed. The interest in this lottery was predictably strong and recouped a considerable sum for the government.

Tattersall's remained in Tasmania until, in 1953, it was established in Victoria where, as in the territories, it was already a household name.

The first lottery administered and controlled by the state was in Queensland in 1916. The legislation banning lotteries was openly defied by the Queenslanders as they sought to raise money for the Patriotic Fund to support the Great War. The legislation was then altered. WA and NSW saw their first legitimate lotteries during the depression of the 1930s, expressly to raise funds for government welfare services. Finally, and with some reluctance, SA entered the scene in 1966. Here is a brief run-down of the types of games running in each state and territory.

Lotto games

This includes Tattslotto as played in Victoria, Tasmania and the Australian Capital Territory as well as Lotto in New South Wales and Western Australia, Sportslotto in Northern Territory, X Lotto in South Australia and Gold Lotto in Queensland. There are slight differences between the games but in all the principle is to pick six numbered, coloured balls which are to be drawn from a barrel of 45 balls (or 44 in NSW). Two supplementary balls are also drawn and are used to make up lesser prizes. Although Lotto as well as all the other games described here are games of pure chance (that is what defines a lottery) there are nevertheless various systems entries which can be filled out to increase player interest and the odds of winning. Playing systems is simply a matter of marking additional boxes on the entry form. It costs extra but is proportionately a better bet for the money. It works like this:

Say you are playing a Systems 7 and the numbers you picked were 1, 2, 3, 4, 5, 6 and 7. For the one extra number you would receive six extra games. See the table over the page.

Note that the more numbers you play on the systems entry the more combinations are possible. Thus a Systems 10 entry sees you playing 210 games and a Systems 18 gives you 18 564 games. Systems games also multiply your winnings because as well as a Division 2

LOTTERIES

Game 1	1	2	3	4	5	6
Game 2	1	2	3	4	5	7
Game 3	1	2	3	4	6	7
Game 4	1	2	3	5	6	7
Game 5	1	2	4	5	6	7
Game 6	1	3	4	5	6	7
Game 7	2	3	4	5	6	7

win, for example, you will win in the lesser Divisions with the other numbers making up the sequence.

Lotto games are drawn twice-weekly on television and are currently the most popular form of lottery, quickly replacing the traditional lottery ticket. This no doubt is largely because of the immediacy of Lotto games and the appeal of seeing the numbers drawn one by one on television. It must be said though that the payout of Lotto, as for all the other forms of lotteries in this chapter, is low, with only about 60% of the revenue earned from the games returned in prizes. Considering that Poker Machines return around 90% to the punters (and even this is only just acceptable when compared to some of the other games in this book) you will see what I mean. Sure, you may just pull off the big one, and for a very small sum of money, but this rake-off in gambling terms means that anyone playing the game long enough will most likely lose 40% of money invested. Incidentally most states return about three quarters of their take to the community in the form of welfare. Most of the other money goes towards operating costs.

One aspect of Lotto to take into consideration is that because you have to share the prize pool with everybody else who has selected the same numbers it is better to deliberately pick numbers not commonly used. The point here is that the odds of any sequence of numbers being drawn are identical to those of any other sequence. In practice most people tend to spread their numbers evenly across the whole slip, as though this is the way the numbers 'should' fall. It is better therefore to go for numbers at the bottom or at the sides, unless you have a strong feeling for certain numbers.

Super 66

Super 66 is played in those states represented by Tattersall's as well as in SA, Qld and WA. It is a game optional to and separate from Lotto but is played on the same form, at additional cost, by way of a random selection of six single-digit numbers on the on-line system. These numbers are printed on a separate slip. Prizes are awarded according to the SEQUENCE of numbers picked at random from a barrel containing only single-digit numbers. Note though that there are several balls for each number. Super 66 has its own prize pool and, like Lotto, it is distributed across the range of winners for that Division.

It appears there has been some resistance to this new game by the public, presumably because they don't yet understand its principles. However it is rapidly gaining ground.

Keno

In those states represented by Tattersall's the game is known as Tattskeno and in SA as Club Keno. For a description of the game and an explanation of the rules see the section on Keno on page 69. The lottery version of the game is identical to that which is played in casinos, the only difference being that prizes are distributed according to the pool of money invested instead of to pre-selected odds. Also there is no maximum payout

> **THE FIRST LOTTERY**
>
> The first public lottery was held in Florence in 1530.

per game. Draws are made every few minutes on a daily basis, except Sundays and public holidays.

Keno is the success story of lotteries in the 1990s. Although only introduced by Tattersall's in 1988 and in 1990 by SA it is already stealing interest from the other forms of lotteries as well as bringing in some additional punters. In some cases it is beating mid-week Lotto sales. In fact the current trend is away from other lottery games and towards Keno, no doubt because of the immediacy of the prizes and the regularity of the draws.

These two factors are the reason that DRAW LOTTERIES are lagging desperately behind Keno with some draws even being cancelled due to lack of sales. The exception here is NSW where these lotteries still represent nearly a quarter of the total sales. It seems jackpot lotteries are largely contributing to this. Queensland is currently pushing to reverse the downward sales trend of its Golden Casket lottery by placing it on-line to make it easier to enter and quicker to see the result. It is significant that in both these states Keno has yet to be introduced.

Instant Lotteries

These are the familiar scratch-and-win tickets sold in all states and territories. Although presently losing some sales to Keno they continue to be a marketing success, mainly, it has been suggested, because of the appeal of instant money: winners can claim their prizes immediately from sales outlets (or lottery office if over a certain amount) without having to wait the two week holding period that applies to some other games. The tickets also make good gifts, a fact not overlooked by some of the authorities who are now producing tickets on themes including special events such as Christmas and Mother's Day. The tickets are sold 'off-line' meaning those states and territories not yet covered by an extensive computer network can still distribute them widely.

An interesting variation on these tickets, called Telespin, is now being introduced into WA. Each ticket contains two panels each comprising one game. The first game is much like a regular scratch-and-win for a maximum prize of $50 000. The second, also a scratch-and-win, will find you, if successful, on state-wide television spinning a wheel for a minimum prize of $10 000 plus the opportunity to win a further jackpot on a second spin of up to $100 000. It is a clever marketing ploy which seems destined to be followed in some form by other lottery commissions.

The Pools

The Pools is based on a weekly round of soccer competitions played in the UK and Australia. The winning numbers are calculated on games which result in a draw with details of the matches being available from lottery agents. Otherwise the game is much like Lotto with numbers selected at random on a coupon and indeed this is the way most people choose to play it. Systems and computer-picked numbers also apply here, as do multiple-week entries and the like. The idea is to pick six winning numbers from a total of 38. All states and territories participate collectively in the Pools courtesy of the Soccer Pools Bloc which has recently taken over administration of the competition. The pools are rapidly declining in popularity and this has the depressive effect of further reducing the funds available for prizes.

There are also other, minor games available in each of the states and territories which for practical reasons will not be covered here. In each case there are brochures available from the lottery agents explaining how they are played. You are not necessarily disadvantaged by

CHANCES OF WINNING LOTTO

What are your chances of winning Division 1 Lotto? For those of you who are mathematically minded the formula is 45c6 or

$$\frac{45 \times 44 \times 43 \times 42 \times 41 \times 40}{1 \times 2 \times 3 \times 4 \times 5 \times 6}$$

And your chances, by comparison, of taking off three winning numbers plus either of the supplementary numbers

$$\frac{45c6}{6c3 \times 37c2 \times 2c1 + 6c3 \times 37c1 \times 2c2}$$

In plain English this works out as follows, given you are playing one game.

Division 1 1: 8,145,060
Division 2 1: 678,755
Division 3 1: 36,690
Division 4 1: 733
Division 5 1: 298
Any Prize   1: 211

Note these calculations are based on there being 45 balls in the draw, which is the case in most states and territories. Also note that if you are playing four games the odds against you are reduced by a quarter; two games, by a half and so on.

entering a minor game, that is for lesser prizes, because you have to remember that there are also less people to claim them. This is an important consideration for those games that distribute a prize pool. However do not make the mistake of thinking that this will increase your chances of selecting correct numbers!

CASINO PROFITS

In 1989-90 Australian casinos in the various states returned $443 million in profits. $80 million of this went to the state governments in tax.

POKER

POKER

Poker, like Two-Up, is something of an institution in Australia, so much so that when Poker Machines were introduced in the early part of this century, Poker symbols soon came to replace the original line of fruit. In fact, if Two-Up hadn't been invented and so readily associated with the Anzac legend, Poker might well be the national gambling game.

Today Poker is played mostly in homes and clubs (many of them illegal), as well as in a number of casinos. Here the house takes a nominal commission from the pot. Estimating the number of people who play Poker regularly is difficult, but its long history and the mere fact that so many people know the rules or something about them is enough to suggest that it is well and truly entrenched.

Nevertheless what most people fail to grasp about the game is that it is primarily one of skill and that finally it is this alone which determines the winner, not the fall of the cards. This is because Poker is about betting. As one champion player put it, he could count on beating an inexperienced player ten out of ten times.

Whereas in other gambling games it is the spin of a wheel, the roll of the dice or even the toss of coins which decides the eventual outcome, in Poker it is the money laid down on the table. This is where psychology comes into it, enough to fill volumes without ever covering every aspect of the game. The truth is that there are as many ways of playing Poker as there are people who play it. Ultimately it is against those people that you will need to plan your strategies. This presents a problem when writing a guide such as this and much ground is left uncovered. Nevertheless there are basic rules of thumb and, as always with gambling games, there are certain calculable odds to be taken into consideration. Later in this section we shall look at those principles as they will at least get you started on the right track. A point worth taking into consideration though is that there are no short cuts or ways of beating the system here. Your only hope against the competition is patience, experience and reason.

Just as there are as many ways of playing Poker as there are people who play it, there are almost as many variations on the game: Draw is the most popular of them but then there is also Stud, Seven-card Stud, Lowball, High-Low and Hold'em, all of which are well established as are others not mentioned here. In addition there are any number of modifications to each of these games, depending on the choice of the group playing or perhaps even the whim of an assertive member. All such variations suggest consequences for the strategist; indeed this is often the point of altering a rule here or there for those who can get away with it. Should 'folded' hands be revealed for instance? Somebody might think so, particularly if there is a new player in the game susceptible to intimidation. Should there be a maximum bet? There are strategies for dealing with this too, even

FIRST POKER GAME

Poker is believed to have originated in the Orient, but it was in the US that it became popular, during the nineteenth century. The first game ever recorded was on a riverboat on the Mississippi. Significantly, one of the gents concerned was a cheat (Poker draws them in their droves), however he only cheated himself on this occasion when instead of dealing himself the intended cards he dealt them to the dupe he was using. The dupe, a young lad, took the pot.

though the rule may be imposed to prevent the stakes getting out of hand.

For now let us concentrate on the basic rules of play. I mentioned earlier that Draw is the standard poker game so it is with reference to this that explanations are made. The other games are sufficiently similar that the comments made here will still apply. This even goes for points of strategy, although reservations and modifications will have to be made as you go along.

Rules of Play — Draw

The game of Draw Poker is played in two parts. First there is the deal and then the draw, with betting after each. The stages of play follow, but note that Draw as played in a casino may have a different system of opening the betting, known as 'blind betting'.

1. The dealer is chosen, most commonly by cutting the cards although any method agreeable to all players is acceptable. By this stage all participants will have put a previously agreed amount of money into the 'pot'. This amount is known as an 'ante'.

2. Once all players have looked at their cards the player to the dealer's left either opens the betting, by putting in more money according to the agreed stakes, or passes to the next player, and so on. If nobody opens by the time the play has returned to the dealer a further ante is added to the pot and the cards re-dealt. If only one person opens that player has won the hand outright.

3. Once the betting is opened all subsequent players must either 'call', 'raise' or 'fold' (see the table of terms) until the play goes around again to the last person who raised. This completes the first part of the game.

4. Players now throw out unwanted cards (if any) and draw replacements from the dealer. A new round of

betting takes place, resuming from where it left off in the last hand. Betting procedure is the same as before, starting with the player who originally opened the betting. Note that players may be restricted as to how many cards can be replaced depending on the house rules.

5. If not all players have folded, leaving one as outright winner (that is, two or more players are still holding cards at the end) the cards are revealed and the player with the highest hand takes the pot. Usually the person who has been seen by the other players shows their hand first. Losing hands may be thrown away without being shown and a player winning outright also has the choice of not showing their hand providing that house rules do not say otherwise. If there is a tie at the end, which does happen from time to time, the pot is split.

6. The deal then passes to the next person on the left and a new game begins. In most cases the group will have decided previously when the session will end to save possible conflict when some wish to disappear with their winnings while others wish to recoup their losses.

Poker Hands

The following are the standard hands of cards from the most valuable Royal Flush down to a humble pair. The total combinations of hands which can be dealt from a 52 card pack amount to a staggering 2 598 960.

Royal Flush

Ace to ten of the same suit, that is A, K, Q, J, 10 all in one suit. Note that for this hand as well as for the others all suits are equal. The probability of a Royal Flush occurring is 64739/1, which means that even as a regular player you may never see one come up.

Straight Flush

Five cards of the same suit. The odds are 72 192/1, or 36 chances in 2.5 million. Also rare!

Four of a Kind

Four cards each of the same denomination. Chances are 4164/1. May appear once or twice in a long session.

Full House

Three cards of one kind and two of another. The odds here are 693/1 but full houses nevertheless appear quite often. If two players have Full Houses the one with the higher denomination of 'three' cards wins. Thus J, J, J, 3, 3 beats 9, 9, 9, A, A.

Flush

Five cards of any kind in the same suit. The probability here is 508/1 so it is also a good hand. Note that four or less cards of the same suit count as nothing and if two people have a Flush the hand containing the highest card wins. If both have the same highest card, Kings, say, the next highest card in each hand is considered and so on.

Straight

Five cards in sequence but of different suits. Again, the higher hand wins and 'busted straights' (four or less cards in a sequence) are useless. The likelihood is 254/1.

Three of a Kind

Three cards of the same kind. Appears regularly with odds of 46/1. Three Kings will beat three 10s for example.

Two Pairs

20/1. Highest pair wins; if pairs are equal, the next highest pair wins, if these are equal, the highest odd card.

One Pair

The odds are 1.5/1 thus they occur with almost monotonous regularity. Unless a high pair comes up it probably isn't worth risking any further stakes on it.

High Card or Bust

Here none of the above categories apply. If the game is being decided between two or more players the highest card wins.

Basic Strategy
— Playing the Odds

As I mentioned at the beginning of this section, Poker is ultimately a game of psychology where the what and how of betting is the key to success rather than the fall of the cards. There are however certain ground rules, acknowledged by all serious players, which must be learnt first. These form the foundations on which you base your play. They fall into three categories: the position where you are sitting in relation to the dealer, the chances of improving your hand after the initial deal and, in regard to this, the worth of the pot and the other bets. You could add to these card-counting and patience — patience especially being the downfall of many an inexperienced player. But let's start with position first.

Position

The basic idea here is that those furthest around from the dealer have the advantage of being able to make decisions based on the players that have gone before them. What they are in effect doing is 'reading' the play. If, for example, you are near to the last on the table and no-one before you has opened you may, given this knowledge, open with say a low pair when otherwise this would be inadvisable. The odds of someone after you (if anyone) having a better hand are less than at the beginning. Thus you may have the chance to 'steal' the pot. Alternatively if you are at the beginning of the table (near the dealer) you have to be aware, at least vaguely, of what the average hand may be (a pair of Kings perhaps amongst a few players) and be careful not to open with anything less.

This covers the opening hand. For the second hand of the game you have to take into consideration that here it is the person following the person who opened in the first hand who is 'under the gun'. A clever player will have anticipated this when moving onto the second round of betting. They will know that if they are near the end this time around they have the opportunity to either fold, at no further cost, or keep going. If they are near the beginning they may have to consider folding.

When we get on to the subject of 'sandbagging' and other psychological tactics we will see that reading the play as described here is not so certain as it at first seems. This can work both for and against you depending how the game is played. A 'Nervous Nellie' early in the opening hand for instance may lure you into the betting when in fact that person is holding a Full House. They will be looking to increase the pot. So be careful. On the other hand you may decide to play the 'Nervous Nellie'.

Cards — Improving On the Draw

Say you are dealt a busted Straight on the first deal, that is, four cards in sequence, of mixed suits. Obviously, this hand is worth nothing as it is, so do you fold, or draw for the fifth card? A number of factors may influence your decision but one of them must be the odds of completing the hand. Your chances of completing the Straight for example are around 5/1 if the completed sequence can be made at either end.

Staking — Betting Against the Pot

To use the example of the busted Straight again, if you know that you have a 5/1 chance of completing the Straight on the next deal you will look at the pot to see what risks you are taking in getting it. This is known as 'pot odds'. Say there is $10 in the pot and thus you can call another player staying in the game for a bet of $1. This will bring you a return of $10 for your $1 which looks good against the 5/1 risk so you may do it. On the other hand if you have to risk $5 to get the $10 you may consider otherwise. An additional advantage of taking the chance is that you may just get the Straight and be in a position to win further bets after the next draw.

Incidentally, the above knowledge may be used by you as part of your betting strategy against other players. A very good way of keeping busted Straights out of the game, thus away from the possibility of others drawing higher than you on the second deal, is to raise the stakes to make it more of a gamble for them. Unfortunately this presupposes that they know better than to bet against 'pot odds' — it is ironic in poker that often the most favourable opposition, at least as far as logical, predictable playing is concerned, is the 'better' player. However you can at least console yourself that the inexperienced player is really a 'non-starter': the odds are well against him or her at the end of the day.

Counting Cards

Poker is always played with one pack of cards which means it is possible to count the cards as they land on

---

DEAD MAN'S HAND

The year is 1876. The place a saloon in Deadwood Gulch. It is night. Wild Bill Hickok is playing Poker with some accomplices when a villain named Crooked Nose McCall sneaks up behind him and shoots him through the back of the head. From that time on the cards Wild Bill was holding as he fell have been known as 'Dead Man's Hand': two Pairs, Aces and eights.

the table, provided you are playing a game that allows at least some cards to be seen. If you are sitting on two Kings, say, and going for a third you will naturally take into consideration the fact that there may be one already out when calculating the odds.

Advanced Strategy — the Poker Face

Everyone knows what a 'poker face' is, it means to be able to control one's expression or gestures so that you do not give anything away. Poker faces have a variety of uses in different situations but in Poker they are central to the game. If you can 'read' other players without their being able to read you then as long as you know how to be prudent with your cards and your betting you are a sure winner, even taking luck into consideration. Thus advanced strategy can be summed up in one word: psychology. 'Bluffing' is a very good example of this but what is perhaps even more important is to know the particular styles of the other players in the group. Any bluffing has to take this into consideration. Unless the other players are either very good and vary their game a lot, or otherwise are very erratic, with some skill in observation you will soon pick up their individual characteristics. And even the very good players will give something away. What about the player who always slams his fist on the table when he fails to improve on the draw? Or this other who has a tendency to bluff? Or the next who makes wild bets whenever they have a particularly successful hand? All very useful information indeed.

Sandbagging

Also known as 'check-raising' (see table of terms for a brief explanation) this is a tactic used to encourage people to bet against your winning hand. The idea is of course to raise the pot as far as possible so that at the end of the game you walk away with the greatest amount of money that you can squeeze out of your hapless opponents. While this is the name of the game — in Poker, you are always looking to capitalize on your winning hands — this particular ploy is considered by many to be unsocial play. It may even be disallowed or at least be subject to certain limitations such as the amount that can be wagered the second time around.

Drawing Cards

Another technique for reading your opponents involves taking note of the cards drawn by each player on the second hand. Two cards drawn, for instance, will suggest that the opposition has Three of a Kind.

But not necessarily. Part of the skill in drawing lies in deceiving the other players into thinking you have better or worse cards than you actually have, or at least throwing them off the track. So in the above example the player may only have a Pair, and a low one at that,

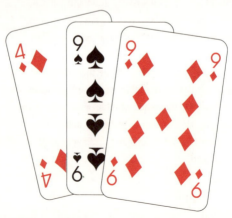

Here the player has retained the four as a kicker.

but they retained a side card, known as a 'kicker', as a red herring. In deciding to keep the kicker the player has taken the opportunity cost of sacrificing the possibility of a Full House, or of improving the chances of Four of a Kind. That too is a tactical decision.

Bluffing

Many of the bluffing techniques have already been discussed during the course of this chapter, such as the one given above in reference to drawing cards, and they may be used for a variety of ends. Here is a sample of them:

1. To give the impression that you have a higher hand than you in fact have, in order to force the opposition out of the game. This is the classic bluffing situation.

2. Given 1, and especially if you have won the hand, you may go to some pains to show your bluff so that the next time you start raising bets others will think you are again bluffing and will raise the stakes against you accordingly. Only this time you are NOT bluffing!

3. To give the impression you have a lower hand than you in fact have. You would do this to keep people interested, the idea being to maximise the pot and therefore your winnings.

In practice though there is much more to bluffing than the simple examples given above and the art is to know the appropriate times for using it. You probably wouldn't bluff against someone who only raises on sure bets, for example, because the chances are you will be done in at the end. It is probably not a good idea to bluff with nothing in your hand either, or against more than one other player. You also don't want to bluff when for one reason or another it is obvious. For a more detailed look at bluffing consult one of the many specialist Poker books available.

Wild Cards

Wild cards introduce variations on the game of Draw Poker to liven up the game by vastly improving the chances of receiving high hands.

Two of the most common variations are known as Deuces Wild and the Bug. In Deuces Wild all twos are counted as anything the player prefers. In the Bug, a card, usually the Joker, may be used as either an Ace or to complete a Straight or Flush. Here all odds given for the various Draw hands are irrelevant. Not even the order of the hands from the most difficult to the easiest holds because with both Deuces Wild and the Bug the rarest hand now is Five of a Kind. Also it is clear that opening hands will have to be higher: in fact right through the game you will have to be aware that the 'average' hand held by the opposition will be a lot stronger. Thus you may consider that three Kings is the minimum required for opening in Deuces Wild and so on. As a matter of course you will also be on the lookout for how many of these wild cards have come up, especially in the case of the Joker since there is only one in the pack.

Jackpots

This is another variation on the game of Draw, this time ensuring that the game is opened with a 'true' hand, that is a minimum of a pair of Jacks. Thus busts or busted Straights for example may not be used. However once the game has been opened the game reverts to the same rules as for Draw and even the player opening with the Jacks may discard them for new cards in the second deal. Also, other players can come in with lower hands after someone else has opened. Make sure if you are opening and you are splitting your pair for new cards in the draw that at the end you have your discard available for others to see — openers caught cheating forfeit their right to the pot.

If no-one is able to open in the first deal a new round of antes are placed in the pot and the cards re-dealt. This time the minimum required is a pair of Queens. If no-one can open still the game converts to Kingpot. After Kingpot it is Acepot, Acepot again (Aces low), twos and so on back to Jackpot. But given the probability that at least a pair of Jacks turns up every hand for a group of players there is little chance that an entire circuit will be completed; a run of three or four non-starts though is possible.

Five-Card Stud

Also known just as Stud this is a form of Poker quite different to Draw, although obviously still based on it. The important changes here are that after the initial card is dealt the others are dealt face up, that there are four rounds of betting instead of two and there is no draw (thus no cards are discarded).

Betting begins after the first and second cards have been dealt (one face down, the other face up) and the opener is the player with the highest card facing. Betting proceeds at this point as for Draw. When completed the third card is dealt to those players who haven't yet folded, then the fourth and fifth. As before, there is a round of betting after each deal with the player holding the best facing cards opening. Thus someone holding the only Pair in the second round will open when in the first round another player may have opened displaying a single Ace.

Stud is a more aggressive game than Draw because it is more open; also because the extra betting makes for higher stakes. Nevertheless basic strategy dictates that to stay in the game you must have at least as high a hand as the opposition. Consequently players tend to fold more frequently. Knowing when to toss in the cards, or when to hold them, is the key to Stud: as usual it is a matter of calculating the odds against you. If for example you are holding a Jack in the 'hole' (face down) and somebody else is showing a King you know already that you are taking a big risk in carrying on. They may have another King in the hole. You are making an even bigger risk if someone else is showing a Jack: your chances of making the pair are markedly reduced.

One similarity with Draw though is that position, cards and pot odds play just as vital a role (see page 116). In this regard if you are sitting near the end of the table and the players behind you with higher cards are betting and raising heavily you would have to consider folding. On the other hand if you are sitting near the end with the same cards but betting before you is tentative or nonexistent you may have the chance to edge in a small bet to test the others. You are then giving yourself the opportunity to improve on the next hand (to get Three of a Kind perhaps if you have a Pair). If betting remains weak from the others you may also have the opportunity to come in bold and brash and 'steal' the pot. Another tip for Stud players is to bet hard if it appears from the cards facing you have the strongest hand. You want to force the others out — especially if your cards only 'appear' strong. Having the fortitude to bluff and see it through is a prerequisite of this game.

Seven-Card Stud

As expected this game is very similar to Five-Card Stud in many respects, the differences arising from the two extra cards dealt. Bear in mind though that for the smart player the differences amount to considerable alterations in match play.

Here two cards are dealt face down, then four face up

Seven Card Stud dealing sequence.

and another face down at the end. There are five rounds of betting, proceeding as for Five-Card Stud, beginning after the first three cards are dealt and then between each deal. To make hands, five cards from the seven are selected. The other two are discarded.

Lowball

There are several versions of this game but in all of them the idea is to score the LOWEST hand. It is therefore Poker in reverse with a bust of 6, 4, 3, 2, A (Aces are low here) off suit being the best hand. On this basic principle the game may be played according to the rules of Draw, Stud, Seven-Card Stud or any of the variations also described in this chapter such as Jackpots or Wild Cards (Kings wild being common). One popular version of Lowball combining at the same time 'high' poker is 'Jacks Back'. On page 122 you will see the rules for Jackpots, Jacks Back is played in a similar fashion with one difference: if Jacks are not made on the initial deal the game reverts to Lowball.

You will remember that, when balancing busts against each other, it is the highest card which normally wins. In Lowball, the lowest highest card determines the winner. It is worth bearing in mind that in Lowball nine-high is about average for a hand, anything higher and perhaps you should fold.

High-Low

This is a particularly popular game for social playing because, like Jacks Back, it combines both 'high' and Lowball poker at the same time, only here it provides players with double the chances of taking a share in the pot. Therefore it invites much participation and betting. Usually the pot is split between the high and low winner.

This game is most often played with Seven-Card Stud although Draw and Stud can also be used. Playing High-Low Seven-Card Stud makes for a fascinating game because with the choice of seven cards you may with the one completed hand have the choice of going for either the high or the low score, depending on the other players' hands and the rules of the showdown. You may also have the choice of going for both the high AND the low scores thus cleaning up the pot from both ends. There are three acknowledged methods of determining the winner(s) at showdown:

1. By allowing the cards themselves to determine the winners. Thus the cards are turned over at the end of the game and the winners selected from each players' best and worst combination.

2. By asking the last better (or if everyone has checked, the one with the highest hand) to reveal his or her nomination of either high or low with everyone else following suit around the table.

3. By each player nominating which way they are betting at the same time. This is usually done with a simultaneous show of chips: one chip indicates 'high', two 'both' and none 'low'.

The first way is quite straightforward, that is, it involves no skill, but the second two constitute games of their own. This is particularly true of the second technique

POKER

TERMS USED IN POKER

Pot the kitty or amount of money wagered by all players on one game

Ante amount placed into the pot by each player prior to the commencement of the hand

Blind Ante when a player is required to bet before the cards have been dealt

Open the initial bet once the first card or cards have been dealt

Check to defer to the next player to open the betting, also to remain in the pot because no one else has bet

Call to match the opening or previous bet

See as above (call) but at the end of the hand

Raise to increase the bet of the previous player

Check-raise to check first then raise next time the betting comes around to you again in the same sequence

Hand a play, comprising a series of bets between each deal

Fold to withdraw from the hand, thus forfeiting any right to the pot, usually by throwing all your cards onto the discard pile

Discards abandoned cards

Draw the basic form of Poker, also to deal replacements for discards

Showdown when players turn over their cards to determine the winner at the end of the hand

Hole card or cards in the face down position in the various forms of Stud where the latter players around the table may change their minds several times before finally making their choice. For this reason it is a little unfair on the early players. The last technique demands skill (the players must still choose which way they are going to go) and is fair as well, probably making it the best of the three. In common practice the player going for both (high and low) must then take off both to win. If not they forfeit their right to both pots.

Hold'Em

Hold'em is very much like Seven-Card Stud except that instead of seven cards being dealt to each player only two are; the hands are completed from another five cards dealt in common to all players. These are known as community cards. Let us say that each player has been dealt their first two cards. A round of betting takes place. Now three cards are dealt out together in what is called a 'flop' and another round of betting takes place. Then the fourth card with a round of betting and then the fifth again with a round of betting. There are in all then four rounds of bets.

Because each player has five cards in common with everybody else betting is usually very close, with the traditional good betting cards (a pair of Aces say after the first two cards are dealt) being no guarantee of success. You have to really study the other possible players' hands here and then plan your strategies. What matters in this game is the potential of making a high hand remembering that any combination of first two cards dealt has the potential to score highly.

BACKGAMMON

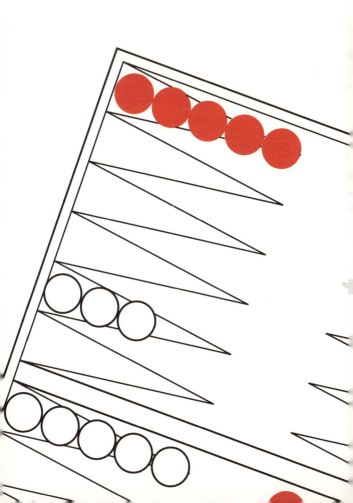

Those who are more familiar with Backgammon as a game of fun, that is without stakes, will probably be surprised to see it here. Nevertheless as a 'gentleman's' form of gambling it has a long history. Indeed in the early colonial Gentleman's clubs that once abounded in Australia it was very popular. If you still remain sceptical, turn to the section called 'Staking in Backgammon' and you will see that this aspect of the game is quite highly developed, demanding a skill of its own not unlike that required for Poker. Today professional Backgammon tournaments are played around the world with substantial prizes.

However the fact remains that it is essentially an intimate game best suited for playing amongst friends. Although considerable skill is required to master the finer points of strategy the rules are nevertheless easy to learn and even an inexperienced player can pip someone stronger with some luck in rolling the dice.

How to Play

Over the page you will see a typical set up of a Backgammon board. Each player has fifteen pieces, seven on one side of the table and eight on the other, which they attempt to move to the side of the board nearest themselves before bearing off. 'Bearing off' is removing the pieces from the board and as we shall see later the player bearing off all their pieces first, wins.

The initial set-up is always as shown over the page, the direction of the arrows indicates which way the pieces move around the board. It is permissible though for both players to move in the opposite direction around the board in which case the board is simply turned around. Each player then has two pieces on the farthest 'point' (position), five on the nearest point on the far side of the table and two groups of five and three pieces on the near

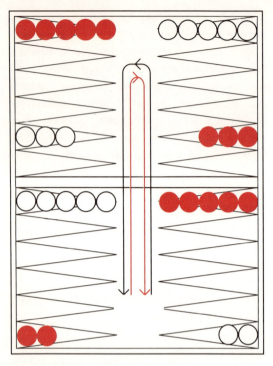

A typical set-up of a backgammon board

side of the table. Of course the two pieces on the farthest point have the longest distance to travel.

What you will also notice here is that in attempting to move the pieces into a position where they can bear off each player is moving in the opposite direction to their opponent. Both are competing then for the right to use the points (which are shared) and as we shall soon see one player may be able to send another's piece or pieces to the Bar (or centre) line to start again. Together these constitute the main challenges of Backgammon. Ignore the colours of the point triangles. They are only to make counting easier.

If the game is to be played for money the staking units

would have been determined before the first throw and the initial bets laid down. For our purposes we will look at the rules of the game here and move on to the betting later.

To begin each player takes a die (there are two used for Backgammon) and throws to see who starts and, if desired, to pick a side or colour although this gives no advantage. A cup is used to throw the dice. After the throw is made, onto the board (if they land on an angle or bounce off they are 'cocked' and thrown again), the player with the highest die uses the scores on both dice to open the game.

Say a 3 and a 5 are thrown; the move is made by either moving one piece three points along the table and another piece five points, or one piece eight points. This is the system used throughout the game. If however a 'doublet' is thrown (for example, two 3s) the player has in effect four numbers to play with $(3 + 3 + 3 + 3)$ and can play them in the following fashion: one piece twelve points; two pieces six points each; one piece nine points and another piece three; or finally four pieces moving three points each. Thus doublets are very good for covering a lot of ground. Note however that if the opponent has two or more pieces on a point (known as 'making' a point) you are prevented from landing there. The reverse is also true, of course. Also note that each number must be able to move in its own right, separately, even where you are combining numbers to make up a total. To make this clearer let's take the roll of a 3 and a 5 again. In order to be able to move one piece a total of eight points you first have to be able to move that piece either three or five points along the board and then on to the eighth point.

Over the page is a sample board, a 'snapshot' of a game mid-way through to demonstrate certain key issues. Here the red pieces are moving clockwise around the table towards the bottom right and the white pieces are moving anticlockwise towards the bottom left.

The first thing you will notice here is the red piece in the centre. This piece has been 'hit' and is sitting on the Bar line. A piece is said to be hit when it is sitting alone on a point and the opposition's piece lands there. Such a piece is known as a 'blot'. Any pieces removed to the Bar line must re-enter the game before that player can move anything else. Now let us assume the red has thrown a 6 and a 4 in an attempt to rejoin the game. As you can see, both these points are made so red will have to miss a turn while white, to keep things simple, moves

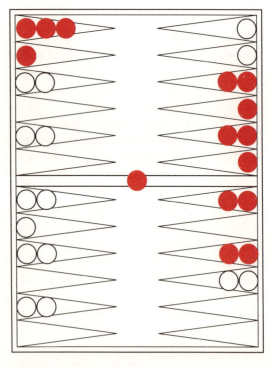

A game of Backgammon halfway through.

a piece a few points on the far side of its table. This time the red throws a 4 and a 5.

The piece is still prevented from moving to the fourth point but on the fifth is a single white. Now it is white's turn to be hit as red moves back into the game and proceeds as normal.

There is no limitation as to the number of pieces that can be placed on the one point and any unoccupied point is available to both players. Pieces must be moved if they can. If, as sometimes happens you can move one piece or another but not both, you must move the higher number.

A player is said to have a 'prime' when they have made six points in a row so that none of the opposition's pieces behind it can move past. Primes often occur towards the end of the game when players have all or nearly all their pieces in their inner area and they are getting ready to bear off.

Bearing Off

Once a player has moved all his or her pieces into the inner area (in the example given opposite the bottom right quarter for the red) they are then able to bear off their pieces to win the game. Quite frequently it happens that both players will be bearing off at the same time with often a desperate race to the finish. However, the mere fact that your opponent is not yet ready to bear off while you are is no guarantee at all of your success because there is still plenty of scope to become unstuck if caught with a blot.

The technique of bearing off goes according to the throw of the dice. If for example a 4 and a 2 were thrown the player would ordinarily bear off those pieces which are that far away from the end of the board (points 1 and 3). However, they are not required to follow this course, and probably wouldn't if they were in danger of being hit. But supposing there were no pieces less than four moves away. In this case two other pieces would have to be moved closer or, if possible, one piece could be moved six points to bear off. On the other hand, if a 6 and a 5 were thrown and all pieces left were on the last four points the pieces furthest from the end must be moved first. Another must is if you throw a number for an unoccupied point between others that are occupied. Here the piece or pieces furthest from the end are to be moved before the others. Doublets are played as before.

Staking

In addition to laying down a basic stake on the outcome of the game, Backgammon also incorporates the use of a doubling cube which allows repeated doubling of the stakes. This idea is unique to the game so we will look at it in some detail.

First the basic stake is agreed on by both players before the game commences. This provides the basis for the doubling. Then if the game is won without the other player bearing off even one piece, or won with the other player still having a piece on the Bar line, the basic stake is increased: doubled in the first case and trebled in the second. Thus the game is said to be worth either one, two or three points at the end. So of course if the basic stake is increased in this way any further doubling by use of the doubling cube further increases the money wagered. By the end of a close game the stakes can be quite high.

The doubling cube itself is similar to a large die with 2, 4, 8, 16, 32 and 64 marked on its sides. Initially, it is placed on the middle of the Bar line with the 64 showing. Here the 64 indicates only that the doubling is yet to commence. It is then turned over when required. It may even be turned over before the game is begun if a doublet (on the playing dice) is thrown for the play-off. This is an automatic doubling unless the players agree otherwise.

Either of the two players can initiate the doubling once the game has started (the cube must be turned over when it is your turn and BEFORE you have thrown the dice) but once it is thus turned over it is subject to the following rules.

Most importantly the other player has the choice of refusing the challenge in which case the game is abandoned. The challenger will take whatever stakes were initially laid down. But since the idea of offering the double is to take advantage of a winning position you consequently have to be careful how you play it. If the game is well and truly in your favour you may only be giving the opposition an 'out'.

Once again you are also surrendering your right to double once you have turned over the cube, at least until the opponent doubles back, because as soon as your doubling offer is accepted the cube is pushed over to their side of the table for their sole use. Naturally, this may also give you an 'out'. You are constantly having to balance and re-balance your relative position during the game in order to play the cube to your best advantage. Experience and some insight into your opposition will be your best guides.

In practice the doubling would never, or hardly ever, get near 64 on the cube. Usually 8, maybe 16, would be as high as it gets and some games don't use the cube at all. The use of the cube often means that games are cut short, sometimes even after only a few throws if one player gets away to a quick advantage.

Finally, there is a variation with the doubling cube, known as the 'beaver', which allows you to double straight back, that is, offering a return double BEFORE that player throws their dice to end the play. The point here is that in doing this you keep your turn with the cube. Players may also agree to settle early where the person losing offers to bow out for part of the stakes. The other player will usually accept because it ensures them of most of the pot.

Playing to Win

The bottom line to successful Backgammon strategy is positioning. While you want to move your own pieces forward as fast as possible you are also thinking of ways to block the other player's moves. Again this is largely a matter of experience as well as on-the-spot thinking but there are various well-known methods of assisting these decisions, some of which we shall look at.

Working the Odds

Below is a table showing the probabilities of landing on any particular point. It is particularly useful in calculating the chances of being able to execute a given aim such as making a point, hitting an opponent's piece or

1	25-11	10	33-3
2	24-12	11	34-2
3	22-14	12	17-1
4	21-15	15	35-1
5	21-15	16	35-1
6	19-17	18	35-1
7	30-6	20	35-1
8	30-6	24	35-1
9	31-5		

bearing off. It is important to know how it works though because as you will see there are times when the odds are reduced. Let us take as our example the number 4, referring to a piece moving four points. Here there are 15 combinations of the two dice that will see this come up out of a possible 36 (6 x 6). See table below.

2 + 2 (2 + 2)	x(1, 2, 3, 5, 6) + 4
3 + 1	4 + 4
1 + 3	1 + 1 + 1 + 1
4 + x (1, 2, 3, 5, 6)	

But what if your opposition has 'made' a point three away? Then you can't throw a 3 + 1, a x(3) + 4 or 1 + 1 + 1 + 1 so you are now looking at 12 combinations. A 42% chance of succeeding drops to 33%. Note that the numbers 13, 14, 17, 19, 21, 22 and 23 cannot be scored but all other numbers up to 24 can. Numbers over 12 are achieved by doublets. Finally, it is worth bearing in mind that there is a 31% chance of any individual number occurring, a 5% chance of any particular combination coming up and a 3% chance of scoring any particular doublet. This will enable you to judge, for example, whether it is worth risking a blot or what your chances are of leaving the Bar line.

Point Counting

This is a technique used particularly in reference to the doubling cube in order to get an idea of how far ahead or behind you are in the game. There are three ways of doing this.

1. Counting the number of points each player has to move to reach their inner boards (the last, home

quarter). The simplest way of doing this is to first cancel out any of the opponent's pieces directly opposite yours on the board.

2. Adding up all the moves required by each player to bear off all their pieces. This is more accurate than the first method but is more suitable to the final stages of the game, for practical reasons.

3. Working out the number of rolls required by each player to bear off all their pieces. This is the most accurate guide of the three but is practical only when each player is down to the last few pieces.

One thing to remember is that the average total of the dice is about eight. Therefore as long as you are ahead by at least this amount in the final stages of the game you have a good case for doubling the cube. Otherwise 16 is considered safe.

Game Plan

There are three acknowledged ways of playing and outplaying your opponent, depending on your relative positions in the game. If you have thrown some high scores early on for instance it is probably worth making a sprint for the finish line. If on the other hand it is your opponent who has the advantage the idea is to block their movements by building up primes. If things are worse still you may opt for a rearguard action. However the idea is always to make as many points as you can to hinder your opponent. At the same time you want to avoid being caught in the same manner.

Sprint

It is generally considered that if a player can make the point second in on the inner table early in the game they are straight away in a good position to take it. The main reason for this is that with two made points on the inner table (with the original held from the set-up) that player has a sound base on which to bring the other pieces home. The other reason is that it may also set up a prime in the event of the opponent trying to move off the Bar line at some stage of the game. Even if a prime isn't established it still restricts the opposition's movements and will quite likely see them hit again. In any case the idea with the sprint is to otherwise ignore hitting and other such strategies for a quick run home.

The Prime

Here the plan is to disrupt the other player's advantage in order to allow yourself the chance to catch up. What you want to do is either hit the other player's pieces or else make as many points as possible so that the opposition's movements are restricted. Say you can manage to hit a couple of their pieces. Taking into consideration that it takes on average three rolls of the dice to move a piece from the Bar line to that player's inner table this gives you three free throws to catch up for each piece hit.

Rearguard Action

This is the most desperate of the three games and the most difficult to play, but if used effectively can throw the odds back in your favour. Here no attempt is made to move your own pieces forward; instead the idea is solely to build up pieces in your opponent's inner side so that as they come around you may have the chance to send them back to the Bar line. Thus it is logical to use this game when your opposition has gone ahead by hitting you first. Any further hits the other player makes against you only frustrates their progress even more as returning pieces have a chance to group in the inner area. Meantime you are trying to steal your own pieces around to your inner table.

This game is even more difficult to pull off if the opponent is wise to your tactics and so delays moving into their inner area or avoids hitting you. If this happens the game could go either way as both players are caught in a battle of wits. A win from this position is quite a coup.

CHEATING

Cheating at games of chance, such as cards, and on racecourses used to be commonplace in bygone eras. But not today. At least not on such a wide scale, thanks to modern technology and a generally tighter security at venues for gambling. Casinos for example are the subject of stringent government controls, for the good reason that governments are depending more and more on revenues taken in the form of taxation. Obviously it is in their interest to keep the party clean. But watch out for 'underground' casinos — here the story is quite different.

Cheating will never be stamped out, of course, be it in the form of a sly wink at the poker table, or a grand scheme on the racetrack designed to rake in thousands of dollars from the bookmakers. Wherever gambling takes place there will always be sharp operators on the lookout for a chance to cheat, as we shall see. Here are some of the better known and more notorious methods.

Cards

Over may be the old days of rootin' tootin' gun-slinging outlaws, yet this doesn't mean that there are no longer any card sharps. Their appearance, and some of their bolder ploys may have changed, but they can be just as deceiving. Their methods include marking the cards and shuffling them so they know where the key cards lie in the pack and then dealing them in their own favour.

Of course there are many other ways of cheating used by sharpers: they may switch the position of certain cards within the pack; they may palm a card and hold it for later use, or hand it straight to a conspirator; they may bring a marked deck of cards into play with identification so ingenious that only they have a hope of spotting them.

How to catch the card cheat? That's a tough one. Be vigilant at the table. Watch the play of strangers to the game (while you're also watching the regulars). And keep on your guard for unexplained, perhaps illogical, happenings. This is really the only way you may ever catch a card sharp, short of hiring your own detective, but it can be reliable enough. Poker, for instance, has its own internal consistency which, if broken, will immediately make itself obvious. The best thing to do in this circumstance is to get up and simply walk away from the game or, if possible, bar that person from any future games. As far as casinos are concerned, any suspect dealings that may once have occurred have been virtually eliminated with the use of the shoe.

Dice

Just as games of chance involving dice go back to the far reaches of history, so too do the crooked ways of throwing them. But, once again, dice games at casinos are now strictly controlled and sharp eyes are constantly on the lookout for cheats. Today dice are designed for accuracy and are locked up when not in use.

However, a few tips may help, especially if you are playing a 'friendly' game. In the event of dice bouncing from a table during play, watch to see that the stickman calls for replacements, thus preventing the possibility of a switch. Be on the lookout for loaded dice. Check them from time to time during the game (without being too deliberate about it) to ensure that their sides are of even and equal dimensions.

When playing Craps, ensure that the shooter is bouncing the dice off the back wall. This practically eliminates sharp players who cheat by throwing the dice — after hours of practice — to their advantage. And finally, if you are at all unsure of the players and/or dice, keep right out of it.

Horse Racing

Cheating involving race horses has provided some amazing stories down through the years, about desperate people taking desperate measures to make money. These tales could easily fill several books — here is just one to give you a feel for the spirit of things.

Grafter Kingsley, a huge man who made and lost several fortunes was, in 1903, the mastermind of one of racing's most audacious scams. Shrewd observers at that time had noticed that two of Kingsley's horses, Harvest Home and Gentleman Jim, which he both owned and trained, won every time he backed them. It seemed uncanny. If the big fellow declared that either horse was a good thing it would romp home; and if he told his friends he didn't fancy the horse's chances it would figure among the also-rans.

The weight factor, as all racing people know, is crucial to a horse's chances. There is a saying that weight will stop a train, the inference being that if it can anchor a train then it can positively buckle a slender-legged racehorse. Yet Kingsley's two horses kept winning even though they were being handicapped with increasingly heavier weights. There appeared to be no limit to the poundage they could handle. This seemed rather odd to race club officials, a complete mystery to handicappers and a severe pain in the hip pocket to bookmakers, who on racedays dreaded the approach of the ever-beaming Kingsley.

The reason for the extraordinary weight-carrying feats of Kingsley's horses was this: Harvest Home and Gentleman Jim were often running with up to two stone less than their allotted weights. At several racetracks in the Newcastle district Kingsley had arranged for tunnels to be dug leading to hide-outs directly underneath the official scales in the weighing rooms, which usually adjoined the jockeys' rooms. Also a peephole was bored at an angle through the wooden floor so that someone in the hide-out could see the scales.

Before the races Kingsley would arrange for a middleman to hire a boy to sleep overnight in the hide-out, and on raceday the modus operandi involved simple arithmetic, nerve and perfect timing. If one of his horses was handicapped at say ten stone, Kingsley would stamp a foot on the floor just before his jockey stepped onto the scales. The jockey's real weight (plus saddle) would be only, say, eight stone, and when Kingsley gave his signal the boy in the hide-out would attack a lump of lead weighing two stone onto the end of a piece of wire, the other end running through a hole in the floorboard and firmly secured to the rear of the base of the scales, where it could not be seen by officials. When the jockey stood on the scales the weight of himself and his saddle and accoutrements would register at ten stone. The horse's race would be run and won, and Kingsley and the jockey would give an encore at the weighing-in, again with the stamping-of-the-foot routine.

This sort of stunt would be very hard to pull off now: the relevant authorities are coming down hard on anyone caught cheating and the technology and effort put into preventing it is formidable. Yet ring-ins are still heard of, when horses are switched at the last minute so that a stronger horse is raced for a weaker one (they are made to look the same), and of course there is the vexed issue of drugs. This is the biggest problem facing the authorities, even though swabs are regularly taken after races.

Other Methods of Cheating

A problem that has recently arisen for the various lottery commissions is the use of 'Systems 45' entries in Lotto competitions. There is actually no such thing as a

Systems 45 entry but the name is used for the practice of covering every possible combination of numbers so that the entrant (usually a syndicate investing thousands of dollars) is therefore bound to win a first division prize. The Australian Lotto Bloc, an organization representing the interests of all state lotteries, is currently working on this problem.

Slot machines are considered to be tamper-proof these days, but there are some who claim that the original one-armed bandits — those with the lever on the side (there are still some around) — can be fixed to land on a winning combination of symbols by 'cranking' the handle. It takes some skill these people say, but it improves your odds dramatically!

And lastly, the time honoured question of Roulette wheel-fixing. This is a thing of the past now as the wheels are manufactured to an extraordinary degree of accuracy and, as already mentioned, legal casinos have a very great interest in keeping the game true (no more buttons under the table to see the ball mysteriously stop in a given hole!). Nevertheless perhaps the most common form of casino cheating occurs when players claim another's chips upon leaving the table. Don't jump to conclusions though: it may be a genuine mistake, especially if the table is crowded. Also watch out for unscrupulous dealers who short-change you to take a cut of the money for themselves. Other dealers may pay out more than the given odds for friends or 'friendly' patrons. Against all this it is worth remembering that casinos employ a whole range of devices such as hidden cameras, secret security staff and many other means which they will not divulge, to prevent cheating.

GLOSSARY AND BIBLIOGRAPHY

GLOSSARY AND BIBLIOGRAPHY

GLOSSARY

Ante In Poker an amount of money put up by each player prior to the commencement of a hand.

Back Men Pieces in the opposition's inner table in Backgammon.

Back to Back A term in Stud Poker when a pair is dealt at the start of a hand, one in the 'hole' and the other face up.

Bar Line Area on the Backgammon board where 'hit' pieces await re-entry to the game.

Blind bet Bet made in Poker without first seeing the cards.

Blot A single piece on a Backgammon point.

Box numbers Numbered boxes in Craps where all COME, PLACE and BUY bets are placed.

Boxer The person conducting the game in Two-Up.

Boxman Supervisor of a Craps game.

Buck Marker showing the point number in Craps.

Bug Card in Poker (usually Joker) used either as an Ace or as a card to make up a Straight or Flush.

Burned card Top card removed from the deck by the dealer and taken out of play.

Card counting To keep track of cards that have already passed from the deck or shoe.

Case Card The final card of a particular denomination, after the other three have already been dealt out.

Check In Poker, to let the opportunity to bet be passed to the next player around the table.

Chip Plastic tokens of varying values used for betting in casinos.

Come out roll Initial throw of the dice by the shooter in Craps.

Complete To place a bet in Roulette which covers every combination around a particular number.

Coup A single play in any casino game.

Croupier The casino employee conducting the game.

d'Alembert Staking system used in Roulette based on either adding or subtracting one unit to a tally after each result.

Daily Doubles Bet in which the winners of two chosen events, often the feature events on a racing program, are nominated.

Dead card Any card out of play in Poker.

Dealer General name for all casino employees conducting games; person in control of the deck in card games.

Double down In Blackjack, to double the stakes after an initial pair is dealt.

Doublet Any throw of a pair in Backgammon.

Doubling cube Over-sized die used when betting in Backgammon.

Draw The standard form of Poker to take a card in Blackjack or Poker.

Each Way bet Bet in which a runner is backed for both a win and a place in the same event.

Edge The percentage of stakes in favour of the house.

Evens Any bet which will pay you the same amount as you have wagered.

Face card King, Queen or Jack in a pack of cards.

Field bet A one roll bet in Craps which wins across a range of numbers showing on the dice.

Formguide Published information on forthcoming racing events so that punters and bookmakers may study the chances of runners.

Hard hand In Blackjack, a hand without an Ace or where the Ace counts as one.

Hardway In Craps, a bet for a total of 4, 6, 8 or 10 rolled with a pair.

Heads A throw of two heads in Two-Up.

Hit In Blackjack, to draw a card; in Backgammon, to send an opponent's piece to the Bar line.

Hole cards In Stud Poker, any cards dealt face down and therefore concealed from the other players.

Home board In Backgammon, the player's inner board.

House Any venue conducting games of chance on its premises.

In the black Odds-against bet.

In the red Odds-on bet.

Insurance Side bet that the dealer will make Blackjack.

Jackpot Accumulated prize-money in Poker machines, Keno and the various forms of lotteries; also a form of Poker in which a pair of Jacks or better is required to open.

Keno Game of chance in which punters attempt to guess the numbers on 20 balls drawn from a barrel of 80.

Kicker Card retained by a Poker player for the purpose of deception when drawing.

Kip A wooden implement used to toss the coins in Two-Up.

Kiss When the coins touch in Two-Up.

Linking Where a bank of Poker machines share a large jackpot prize pool.

Live card Any card yet to be dealt.

Lotto Game of chance in which the punter attempts to pick the numbers on six to eight balls drawn from a barrel.

Marker A card which indicates where the last deal is to be made from a pack.

Miss-out A losing throw in Craps.

Natural An Ace plus any other card with 10 value in Blackjack; two card hand of 8 or 9 in Baccarat; come out throw of 7 or 11 in Craps.

No dice An illegitimate roll of the dice.

Odds A throw of a head and a tail in Two-Up; the price given by a bookmaker or house; the chances of a given event occurring.

Odds against Where the probability or bet is at less than even chances.

Odds on Where the probability or bet is at greater than even chances.

One roll bet Type of bet in Craps made on just one throw of the dice.

Outer board A player's far side of the board in Backgammon.

Pat hand In Poker, where a player retains the whole hand without drawing.

Payout Percentage of takings returned to punters in games of chance.

Place bets A type of Craps bet on a particular number, shown in boxes across the top of the table; in horse racing, a bet made for a place rather than for a win.

Point One of the 24 divisions in Backgammon; the numbers 4, 5, 6, 8, 9, 10 in a particular Craps bet.

Pools Type of game in which the punter attempts to predict the number of drawn matches in a combined round of UK and Australian soccer.

Pot In Poker, the kitty.

Proposition bets Any bet from the central box in Craps.

Quinella TAB bet in which the punter attempts to nominate the runners finishing first and second in the same event.

Rail bird Spectators standing behind the action in a casino game.

Raise To improve on someone's bet in Poker.

Right better Player betting that the shooter will pass the Win line in Craps.

Running Doubles Bet in which the punter attempts to pick the winners of two events.

Salle privée Room reserved in casinos for those who bet large amounts.

Seven-out In Craps, when the shooter loses by rolling a 7.

Shoe Box used to hold the cards in Blackjack or Baccarat.

Showdown When all remaining players in a hand of Poker reveal their cards.

Sleeper In Roulette, a number that hasn't appeared for a long while.

Soft hand A hand in Blackjack where the Ace is counted as 11.

SP (or Starting Price) bookie An unlicensed, or 'off course' bookmaker.

Spinner The person holding the kip in Two-Up.

Split In Blackjack, to separate a pair when dealt as the first two cards and play each as a distinct hand.

Stand When a player draws no further cards in a game of Blackjack.

Stand-off A tied result in which all bets are frozen until the next hand or throw.

Streak A run of consecutive winning or losing bets.

Super 66 An additional game on the Lotto coupon in which six single-digit numbers are drawn for the punter at random. It has its own prize pool.

Superfectas TAB bet in NSW in which the first six horses across the line must be nominated.

Sweeten the pot In Poker, to add further money to the stakes.

Systems entry Option in Lotto which allows additional numbers to be marked to create a greater range of combinations.

Tails A throw of two tails in Two-Up.

Trifectas As for quinellas except that you must nominate the first THREE placegetters.

Way bets A combination bet in Keno.

Wild card In Poker, deemed by the holder to be of any value or suit.

Wrong better A Craps player who bets the shooter will not pass the Win line.

BIBLIOGRAPHY

Doyle Brunson, *How I Made a Million Dollars Playing Poker*, B & G Publishing 1978

Peter Charlton, *Two Flies Up a Wall*, Methuen Haynes 1987

Lewis Deyong, *Playboy's Book of Backgammon*, Playboy Press 1977

Charles Einstein, *How To Win At Blackjack*, Gambler's Book Club, Las Vegas 1975

E. Lennox Figgis, *Gambler's Handbook*, Hamlyn 1976

Virginia Graham & C. Ionescu Tulcea, *Casino Gambling*, Van Nostrand Reinhold 1978

Oswald Jacoby & John R. Crawford, *The Backgammon Book*, Macmillan 1970

W.I. Nolan, 'Facts of' Series: *Roulette, Baccarat, Blackjack, Craps* Gambler's Book Club 1970s

John O'Hara, *A Mug's Game*, New South Wales University Press 1988

John Scarne, *Scarne's New Complete Guide to Gambling*, Simon & Schuster 1975, Constable 1975

John Scarne, *Scarne's Encyclopedia of Games*, Harper & Row 1973, Constable 1975

David Sklansky, *Hold'em Poker*, Gambler's Book Club, Las Vegas 1976

David Spanier, *The Gambler's Pocket Book*, Mitchell Beazley Publishers Limited 1980

L. Taetzsch, *Winning Methods of Bluffing and Betting in Poker*, Drake Publisher's Inc. 1976

E.O. Thorpe, *Beat the Dealer*, Blaisdell 1962

Chet Wander, *Gin Rummy*, Holloway House 1978